The War against the Beavers

The War against the Beavers

Verena Andermatt Conley

University of Minnesota Press
Minneapolis / London

This book describes the author's experiences while living in the North Woods. It reflects her opinions and personal impressions, and should therefore be considered a story rather than a factual account. Details and descriptions of individuals have occasionally been modified.

Copyright 2003 by the Regents of the University of Minnesota

Published by the University of Minnesota Press
111 Third Avenue South, Suite 290
Minneapolis, MN 55401-2520
http://www.upress.umn.edu

Library of Congress Cataloging-in-Publication Data

Conley, Verena Andermatt, 1943–
    The war against the beavers / Verena Andermatt Conley.
      p.   cm.
    ISBN 0-8166-4218-4 (acid-free paper)
    1. Boundary Waters Canoe Area (Minn.)—Description and travel.
2. Vermilion River Region (Minn.)—Description and travel.   3. Conley, Verena Andermatt, 1943–   4. Country life—Minnesota—Boundary Waters Canoe Area.   5. Log cabins—Minnesota—Boundary Waters Canoe Area.   6. Natural history—Minnesota—Boundary Waters Canoe Area.
7. Beavers—Minnesota—Boundary Waters Canoe Area.   8. Boundary Waters Canoe Area (Minn.)—Biography.   9. Vermilion River Region (Minn.)—Biography.   I. Title.
    F612.B73 C656 2003
    917.76'7—dc21

            2003001346

Printed in the United States of America on acid-free paper

The University of Minnesota is an equal-opportunity educator and employer.

12 11 10 09 08 07 06 05   10 9 8 7 6 5 4 3 2 1

For Tom

Contents

Acknowledgments

I WOULD LIKE TO THANK all those who have shown interest in these stories from the North Woods and who have given me invaluable help and suggestions reading and editing earlier versions, especially Prebble Eklof, Regina Sadono, and Ruth Quade. I would like to thank those who have helped with the preparation of the manuscript at various stages, Francine Latil and Michael Tan. I am especially grateful to Doug Armato of the University of Minnesota Press for his continued encouragement and support. I would like to thank above all Tom, my faithful companion in these adventures. To him this book is dedicated.

A Cabin in the Wilderness

Growing up in Europe, I dreamed for many years of the great American wilderness. My childhood was spent reading romantic tales of Native American cultures, of life in the forest, of hunting and gathering, of traveling on mighty rivers in birch bark canoes or of braving winds and waves on stormy lakes while trying to escape from humans or wild animals. Many nights I huddled under the covers with a flashlight, devouring books by Karl May, a popular late-nineteenth-century German author whose colorful stories about life in the American West with Chief Winnetou, Old Shatterhand, and Old Surehand fired up my youthful imagination. I held my breath when reading about battles and true friendships between Native Americans and trappers, about riding horses bareback and blazing trails through the impenetrable wilderness. Passages relating how the early trappers made hats out of beaver pelts and roasted the paws of bears over open campfires left indelible impressions.

The vast forests described by May and other writers were in stark contrast to those on my own continent, which, according to textbooks, had been tamed by the end of the ninth century. The forests I knew were largely managed. Brush was kept neatly in check; wildlife was almost extinct so that deer and squirrels caused sensations. Nicely designed inns with parasoled tables completed the picture of these manicured forests. In the stories I read of distant adventures, however, forests were thick and wildlife abounded. The weather was often violent. There were blizzards in winter and fierce electrical storms in the summer that caused fires. Animals could become threatening, too. I read about bears tearing down doors to trappers' cabins, of beavers sinking their teeth into human flesh to defend their territory, and of lone wolves preying on tired, unsuspecting pioneers.

When I finally reached American shores, I discovered that these tales belonged to another age. Wilderness existed, but it was entirely changed. At the suggestion of friends, I complemented my childhood reading with meditations by Sigurd Olson, John Rowlands, Arne Naess, Dorothy Moulter, Helen Hoover, and others whose reflections added to the feelings conveyed by the earlier adventure stories a sense of peace, harmony, and rediscovery of nature away from the encroachments of a rapidly accelerating technological civilization. The contemporary wilderness appeared to have lost none of its appeal. It still provided humans with challenges but also enabled them to experience a sense of oneness with creation and to reconnect with a heightened sense of existence. After reading and hearing these new tales, I was eager to explore the American wilds and especially the North Woods.

My spouse, Tom, more than shared my yearning. Somewhat uncharacteristically for a New Yorker, he had a special taste for outdoor life. Like me, he had derived his sense of the outdoors from books, until the day, that is, when he embarked with a friend on a trip to Quetico, the Canadian wilderness just north of Minnesota. From there he had returned with so many stories that they filled many evenings of our early years together. If my childhood tales of ambush, battles, and roasting bears' feet over open fires in the forest were vanquished, Tom had many others, detailing breathtaking vistas of tall trees and sightings of moose.

He spoke of treacherous rapids, back-breaking portages, and exhausting episodes of paddling against mighty head winds. I was in awe when he recounted scaring away bears that had developed a sudden yen for camp food, shivering in his sleeping bag under star-filled skies, hearing the distant cry of a loon, and the splendor of autumn days when the rays of the sun were shining obliquely through the mist rising from smooth, glittering waters in which beavers lay so still, they could easily be mistaken for floating logs. He was determined to repeat these experiences and wanted nothing more for us than to have our own little place in the woods.

Fate seemed to be on our side when, for professional reasons, we moved to Minnesota, the gateway to much contemporary wilderness. We spent our first years there paddling and camping on Wisconsin rivers whence we emerged with tales of wet tents, capsized canoes, crying children, harried parents, impressive lightning storms, delirious sunshine, exhilarating swims, and other intense sensations. Yet Tom and I continued to dream of having a place where we wouldn't have to book space two months in advance but where we could really come to know nature by living with it.

It would be several years before our dream came true, and by then our children were grown and away at school. One snowy day, a friend called to tell us of a retiring couple who wanted to sell their "dream place" in the North Woods, just south of the Canadian border. We were ecstatic. We called the Morrows, and they told us that they had two small seventy-five-year-old log cabins on a sizable tract of forestland. The property, we were informed, bordered the Vermilion River at the western edge of the Boundary Waters Canoe Area Wilderness (BWCAW) in northeastern Minnesota. They were eager to sell and suggested we go and take a look at it. Tom and I were floating on a cloud. Two small cabins in the wilderness with more than a hundred acres of our own forest. It was too good to be true.

Tom, forever the researcher, dragged out a couple of atlases. He laid them on the kitchen table and we pored over the maps.

The place was easy to find. It was, the Morrows had informed us, in a small community of two hundred people, spread over ten square miles, centered on a post office and several taverns, one of which would later go out of business as a result of a community vendetta and eventually be reborn as a wilderness outfitter. The township consisted of some old homesteads from the turn of the century, especially along the river and, on the county road, some pieced-together shacks and derelict trailers that would sink into the ground before any realtor could put the coveted word "Sold" over the lopsided "For Sale" signs. A couple of resorts, one on the river and the other on a neighboring lake, and a few new cabins completed the scene. The property was on the north side of the Laurentian Divide, where rivers flow to Canada's Hudson Bay, and only a few miles from the chain of lakes along the border.

The double status of the Vermilion as wilderness and historic river made my imagination run wild. I would live on the very same river, I thought, on which the voyageurs, those Frenchmen with the funny woolen caps, paddled in huge canoes at top speed from Montreal to Fort Frances. Sometimes they even ventured all the way down to the confluence of the St. Croix and Mississippi Rivers and back. They traveled by way of the border lakes, enduring inhuman conditions while singing songs and smoking their pipes in rest places called posées (pronounced *pouzay*), a term canoers still use to designate the simple wooden frames along portage trails against which one can lean one's canoe. I would be living on an eighteenth-century voyageur route that was two thousand miles long. From my front door I could be connected downriver to a chain of lakes, to Montreal, Europe, and beyond. I would live on the river where Native Americans had canoed for centuries, where the Chippewa fought and pushed out the Sioux, where beavers, bears, and wolves abounded. The legend in the atlas informed us that the countryside, part of the Laurentian Shield, had been carved by glaciers, which gave the terrain its hills and lakes, rocky points and innumerable waterways.

The appeal was enhanced by the fact that our prospective land was near the BWCAW, which, with more than one million acres, was truly one of the few remaining untamed parts of the country. There had been some legislation since the early years of the century that had set aside the land for recreational purposes, but the Boundary Waters Wilderness Act had not been ratified until 1973 under the renewed desire for preservation. Dorothy Moulter's cabin had originally been located there, though, like Thoreau's hut near Walden Pond in Massachussetts, it had been moved. Moulter's cabin was now in Ely, one of the major entry points to the Boundary Waters, where it served as a museum and landmark.

Conservation had begun in the early twentieth century after successive waves of trappers, fishermen, loggers, and then farmers, some of whom originally had traded and intermarried with, but then largely displaced, the Native Americans, were depleting the land of its resources. Logging around the turn of the century, subsidized by America's "first families," the Rockefellers, the Weyerhaeusers, and others, had felled most of the first-growth white pines that once covered the area. Concerned by the cutting, some folks with vision put early conservation efforts in place in the area of the North Woods now occupied by the Superior National Forest, of which the Boundary Waters area was a part. The national forest, in which our cabins were located, was created and put under federal protection half a century before the passing of the Boundary Waters Wilderness Act. In a sense, Tom declared, the wilderness we were buying into was, for the most part, no longer original. This state of things confirmed those who claimed that nothing was original in the first place. Nonetheless, vegetation had grown back and, although there were many more aspens now than pines, the trees in the area once again stood tall.

The river itself, we learned from a book about canoeing in the Western Boundary Waters, flowed out of Lake Vermilion, one of the numerous area lakes with several hundred miles of shoreline. It emptied itself twenty-two miles farther north into one of the border lakes on the voyageur route. The river's topography was said to be varied. Some rocky shores with tall pine trees and ridges covered with aspen and spruces alternated with reedy marshes. Several spots with treacherous rapids, cliffs, and some rather long and arduous portages made it a difficult river to canoe and would give those who were brave enough a greater chance for solitude.

I paused and looked through the window of our city house, out over the wintry landscape. I could already see myself drinking coffee while mist rose from crystal-clear waters or admiring sunsets behind towering pine trees. I heard warblers singing in the thickets and pictured us sitting in twin Adirondack chairs surveying the scene. I saw us gliding down the river in a canoe in complete silence, except for the sound of our rhythmic paddling, the eerie call of loons and the occasional splash of a beaver . . . Here was the chance of a lifetime. Our dream would come true.

A couple of days later, we jumped into our car and, with the help of a detailed map and written instructions graciously furnished by the Morrows, made our way north to look at the place. "Head north on the Voyageur Highway. Go past the sign with the large bluegill, turn right, go across the railroad tracks, continue straight until you come to the Vermilion River, cross the bridge, eventually turn onto a dirt road, continue past the only other house on this stretch of the river, then drive up a hill and follow the dirt road that looks like a Vermont road [Tom and I envisioned the path in summer as green, mysterious, and with overhanging trees] for about two miles . . ." While I read the directions, Tom executed them at the wheel of our truck. On the day of our scheduled visit, though it was only early December, the countryside was quite forbidding. A recent snowfall had blanketed the region with more than a foot of snow. When we arrived at the bottom of the hill, it looked impregnable. Prudently, we left the truck by the side of the road and decided to go in on cross-country skis, brought along just in case, on the snow-covered "Vermont road."

This was no easy feat, especially during the initial hilly part— a sharp incline where our slow progress was offset by incidents of dramatic regress. During the last part, we had to "schuss" down between tall spruces that seemed always to be in the wrong place at the wrong time, toward the cabins and the river. An icy wind was blowing relentlessly from the North. I pulled down the hood of my jacket against the bitter cold, leaving only a small opening for my eyes. We stumbled, rather than glided, into what we hoped would soon be our "dream place." We took a good tumble or two more, each time leaving a large dent in the snow. Finally we emerged from the thick forest and saw the two little cabins made of hand-hewn logs stained dark brown, one in the woods and one just on the edge. Each had a steep shingled roof—I already pictured plumes of smoke rising from the chimneys—and an enclosed porch that was shuttered for the winter. Farther away, we saw the vast expanse of the frozen river extending beyond a field and disappearing on the horizon between rolling hills covered with dense forest.

Eager to see the inside of the cabins, I removed my skis outside the door of one of them only to sink into a snowdrift almost to my waist. Uttering some unkind words, I struggled to get free while Tom, with rapidly freezing ungloved fingers, unlocked one of the screen doors. Our good spirits returned. We would have real log cabins, on a historic river, near one of the national wilderness areas. What more could we want?

The inside of the first cabin was quite dark and cold in the midafternoon of this wintry day. Once we were accustomed to the darkness, we were able to make out a large room, with another, presumably a bedroom, hidden behind a partition. Although larger pieces of furniture were covered with old sheets, and many smaller items, all clearly identified with the bold black strokes of a marker, were piled up on a table in the middle of the living room, it was easy to see that the cabin was immaculate. I already pictured the scene in the summer. I could smell the freshly waxed floors, see the shining windows through which ample sunlight would flow, big red-and-white comforters on the rough wooden beds. Growing all around the cabins I imagined radiant wildflowers, planted from a box of Johnny's Seeds I had spotted on one of the shelves. The flowers would be offset by the pruned Colorado spruces and finely groomed trails that wound around and beyond the cabins.

The Morrows did not believe in modern conveniences. There was no electricity, no running water, and only a pair of simple outhouses. An old, bright-red generator and an archaic mower were the only gasoline-powered engines on the property. To our surprise—and my delight—there *was* a telephone, essential because of a family member's medical condition. Yet with their tidiness inside and around them—quite a contrast to our tents, I remarked—the cabins truly felt as if they had been built in a pristine wilderness. This feeling was enhanced by shelves of neatly aligned books with such titles as *The Return of Eden, The Healing of Mind and Body, Yoga for Beginners,* and *Organic Foods.* Clearly, the wilderness had undergone some major changes since Karl May wrote about mystical friendships and life-threatening adventures. These cabins would be a place for adventure, to be sure, but also for the restoration of mind and body; here, weary city dwellers could escape from the stress of civilization and commune with nature.

On the way out, we inspected the pictures on the wall. One featured a map of the area drawn by a child. A couple of hand-written Indian sayings about peaceful and harmonious relations between humans and nature adorned its edges. On the other side of the door, I spotted several animal pictures featuring the local species: deer, bear, and beavers. I had recently read that by the end of the nineteenth century, the beavers had been trapped almost to extinction but were now, after years of protection, making a comeback. My heart went out to those lovable creatures, which I knew primarily from the Nature Channel but which, soon, I would get to see in their natural habitat. If need arose, I would offer them shelter. I would make our place into a haven for them all.

In the corner, an old, blown-up black-and-white photograph with yellow smudges showed a barren landscape divided by a dark, winding, vertical band. To my inquisitive glances, Tom replied that this was an aerial picture of our land-to-be, taken in the 1930s when it had been logged for a second time. The dark band was the river. I suddenly had a queasy feeling. So this was our wilderness. It had first been trapped out by the voyageurs before being logged repeatedly. Wistfully, Tom added that another tree harvest was most likely due in about twenty years or so. A "cycle," he declared, was roughly sixty to eighty years. This was unwelcome news, but it seemed a long way off, so I quickly overcame my uneasiness and forgot about the unpleasant prospect.

Once outside, we decided to ski along the partially frozen river, down to a large, reddish boulder deposited there during a distant ice age. While following a narrow snowy path, I glanced up at the slender aspen trees whose barren branches were swaying in the breeze. When I looked back down at the base of the trees, I noticed that many of the gray and white trunks had chicken wire wrapped around them. When he saw my puzzled face, Tom smiled and quoted a bumper sticker he had seen: "Kill a beaver, save a tree!" A shock ran through my body. How could he think that was funny? He reiterated that under protection, the beavers were making a comeback and were beginning to take over every available space. They had a special liking for aspen, he added jokingly. I failed to be amused and became quite indignant. How could he malign these cute little animals?

By now, we were halfway out to the rock and had reached a grove of balsam trees. The area was dark and silent. The trees stood so close together that there was hardly a trace of snow on the ground. A thick layer of needles muffled the sound of our footsteps. Under the trees, almost like a subcanopy, a number of moss-covered tree stumps roughly two feet high looked like sharpened pencils. Tom's earlier explanation helped by distant memories of Walt Disney movies suddenly revealed to me that this was the work of beavers. A stand of aspens had been felled by beavers a decade or so ago, and, in its place, balsam had grown. It all had happened a long time ago, and I did not give it much thought. I lifted my skis and headed in the direction of the reddish boulder, a sign of stability and permanence.

Little did I suspect when I finally reached the big rock and looked back along the river at what I already saw as *our* wilderness, that, before too long, I would *have* to clarify my thoughts not just on the subject of beavers, but on nature itself. On that very first wintry day, when I made pronouncements about beavers and trees, as a city person and total rookie in the woods, I had no idea that during a decade in the North Woods, my philosophy regarding the peaceful coexistence of animals, humans, and nature would be tested. I would experience life in two old log cabins with moments of intense pleasure conveyed by the sights, sounds, and smells around me. I would indeed encounter wild animals, storms, and plagues of insects. My sense of a pristine wild would be completely altered when I found myself engaged in a war with beavers and a dispute with loggers from which I emerged with a new love for the animals and a transformed sense of wilderness.

Everything in the natural world was interrelated, but there was no real harmony. Every order was temporary and changing constantly. Many of the changes were due to natural causes, such as storms, fires, droughts, or insect plagues. With increasing human intervention, the speed and magnitude of change were greatly accelerated. There were, indeed, natural catastrophes, but it was mainly human pressure on the environment—from logging to urban encroachment—that produced sudden changes and made nuisance animals out of beavers and other animals. Our decade in the North Woods would give me not only the adventures and pleasures I had been hoping for but also a greater awareness of the fragility of every order and the need to tread lightly.

That day, however, we did not pursue those thoughts. Eager to buy into our dream, we called the Morrows as soon as we arrived back home and told them we were ready to commit. So enthralled were we that it never even occurred to us to check for rotten logs, bad roof shingles, lack of insulation, or other practical details. A couple of months later, we signed the papers and the place was ours.

PART I

Babes in the Woods

Heading for the Wilderness

ONE SUNNY AFTERNOON IN EARLY JULY, we drove through the North Woods with the help of the same detailed map that had guided us in the winter. After crossing the river and passing the house at the foot of the hill where lived a local couple, Mike and Lonnie, we reached the steep hill with the mossy "Vermont road," lined by aspen, spruce, and some pine and maple trees. The place was unrecognizable on this balmy summer evening. Where slender tree trunks had swayed in the cold wind on snow-covered ground, all was now lush green. Thick underbrush was everywhere, and giant ferns bordered the overgrown road. Tom charged the hill, zigzagging between bumps and rocks, as if he were on a drunken chase. After a couple of miles, we arrived at the weather-bleached wooden gate and parked our truck on a grassy knoll. Nearby stood a wooden half-barrel in which yellow and dark red marigolds—perhaps somewhat out of place in the wilderness— were glowing in the last rays of the evening sun.

Although we had closed on it, it was agreed that the Morrows would hand over the place to us in person. We headed down toward the river and the cabins where they were expecting us.

The property, we had learned, consisted of one hundred fifty acres of forest and a field. It had more than two miles of frontage along the Vermilion River. The two log cabins, built by early Eastern European settlers, had been refurbished, but their primitive appearance had been preserved. The Morrows and their children were purists. They had rebuilt the place under the spell of wilderness.

After a few hundred yards, we passed the "red" cabin, which was nestled among the trees on the hill below the grassy parking space. We continued toward the "white" cabin—that's how the Morrows had decided to distinguish the two structures, though they both seemed to be the same dark-brown color. The "white" cabin was slightly below, on a small promontory with an arresting view of the vast expanse of the river that disappeared between two ridges on the far-off horizon.

We were welcomed by Rob, a trim man in his early sixties, and Louise, a slender woman in her fifties with graying curls and a wide smile that matched the dimensions of her heart. Almost on tiptoes, we entered the screened porch. We were late as usual, and almost immediately the couple asked us to sit at the impeccably refinished wooden drop-leaf table. The evening breeze was blowing softly; Japanese chimes, a souvenir of one of Rob's business trips, tinkled faintly. A smell of sweet incense, a tribute to Louise's Far Eastern philosophical interests, hung in the air, and, completing the multicultural experience, strains of Mozart were now coming from a Canadian station on the battery-operated radio inside the cabin. Louise began serving her homemade hummus as a first course. Tom and I sat quietly, taking in all the sensory experiences. I was in bliss.

A loud noise that sounded as if someone had thrown a big rock in the water interrupted the conversation, but there was no other human in sight. Noting my puzzled look, the Morrows laughed. It was the sound of a beaver tail, they explained. The slapping of the tail served as a warning sign to other members of the colony. Yes, there was a sizable beaver lodge at the foot of the small promontory on which the cabin stood. It had been there for more than a decade. The beavers had "taken down" quite a few trees, but their logging operation had actually improved the view. The Morrows had tried to discourage the population from expanding by planting along the shore various bushes and trees, such as red and white pines, which did not agree with the beavers' delicate palate. I remembered the wire-wrapped trees and the stumps I had spotted during our first visit. Yet the jolly tone of our hosts seemed to preempt any thought of threat and gave the beavers the status of charming and desirable neighbors.

After a few moments of silence, the Morrows started talking again. Clearly, they had trouble letting go of the "family place" in which they had invested so much labor and emotion. They wanted to make sure we would "do it right." Although they were mainly interested in talking about their feelings for the property, a previously hidden, pragmatic side also prompted them to "talk shop," and they both held forth at length. Savoring the red Bordeaux wine we had brought for the occasion, we listened to the couple's sentimental but also increasingly practical descriptions of the property they were handing over to us. Rob began by briefing Tom on the mechanics of the cabin, which revolved especially around the seasonal opening and closing ceremonies. Windows had to be changed, I heard, and oil drained from the two machines. Having perfected the art of business in Japan, Rob clearly showed all the signs of a well-organized man. Looking obliquely at Tom while exchanging niceties, I kicked his shin, amused at the thought that henceforth he, too, would have to be organized.

Rob was by now reciting a list of items that required attention. The Jari was one of his favorite objects in which he had invested particular care. A bright blue four horsepower mower with an impressive sickle-bar cutter, the Jari could cut through brush as well as trees—as we would soon find out the hard way—and even human limbs. I shuddered. This was not the kind of adventure I had imagined. The mower would enable us to keep our little piece of wilderness "habitable." With it we would be able to maintain a patch of "lawn" around the cabin near the river, though we would never, Rob added laughingly, be able to compete with our neighbors. Short-cropped grass was a sign of status in the North Woods, where the battle between nature and culture began anew every day. Trimmed grass would keep the mosquitoes down and give us a spot to put our chairs so that we could watch the river and the wildlife.

Rob impressed on Tom that all water had to be removed from the pipes before the first freeze. All overhanging branches had to be cut back as resin tended to damage roof tiles. The paths around the cabins were to be covered with woodchips to prevent harm to the tree roots. Rob's high-pitched, slightly nasal voice droned on and on. No longer exchanging ironic glances, we had become quite pensive. I had imagined romantic canoe trips on sky-blue waters and picnics under majestic pine trees. I had seen myself watching birds and sighting bears, spending lazy evenings in deck chairs sipping wine. I had pictured myself meditating on humans and nature while ambling down unspoiled forest paths. Inspired by my recent readings on communing with nature, I had visions of recovering some sense of wholeness that had been lost to our mechanized lifestyle, a feeling confirmed by the Morrows' own library. Had we been duped? Had we simply bought a work farm? And this was only half of it.

If the grounds were Rob's domain, Louise reigned supreme on the inside. Her spiritual penchant did not prevent her from running an impeccable household. I paled and felt thoroughly inadequate when I heard that folded plastic covers, bags, glass jars, cardboard boxes, all labeled with masking tape, were an absolute necessity for organizing the cabin. Louise instructed me where to put each object, how to cover it with which plastic sheet so as to keep the critters out, and urged me to take mental notes.

Louise's hummus had by now been consumed. It was followed by a chicken and wild rice casserole. Tom and I were thoughtfully chewing our dinner and nursing our bottle of Bordeaux, which, luckily, the Morrows declined to share with us. My anxiety level subsided somewhat with the glow of the wine, and I was able to become aware of the environment. The litany of seemingly endless directions was interwoven with the rustling of aspen leaves in the evening breeze, the faint chirping of birds at the handmade wooden feeder mounted on a pole in front of the cabin, and the recurring slapping of beaver tails on the swift-moving waters of the river below. The noises helped keep my vision alive.

It was late, and the reflection of the moonlight revealed the V-shaped wake of a couple of beavers crossing the river when Rob, equipped with a strong flashlight that cast eerie, dancing shadows among the trees, showed us up the steep, narrow path to the "red" cabin, where we were to spend our first night in the great North Woods. We entered the guest cabin through the porch. Several oil lamps gave the cabin a radiant gleam. The fresh cool air flowing in through the large screened windows helped dispel my disquiet. I felt happy again as I finally nestled in under the long-anticipated checkered covers, stretched tautly over an old wooden bed. I listened to a faint crackling and stomping in the nearby woods, but, filled to the brim with new sensations, I soon drifted into a heavy sleep.

The shrill sound of Rob's bear whistle awakened us the following morning. The whistle was made to scare bears off, Rob had explained the night before. He assured me, when he saw my startled look, that it produced instant, infallible results. We rose and put on our jeans and new flannel shirts so that we'd at least look the part before ambling down to the lower cabin. We followed Rob's instructions and took utter care to tread lightly. On the porch, a crisp, blue checkered tablecloth with matching napkins covered the drop-leaf table, and a few handpicked black-eyed Susans in a white vase completed the picture-perfect log cabin look. With help of the smell of fresh coffee, the taste of homemade bread, raspberry jam, and the sweet odor of incense, I overcame my fears and recaptured the feeling of having arrived in a wilderness paradise. At long last, we had found the path that led to our dream cabin in the North Woods.

After breakfast, Rob and Louise gave each of us an additional private tour with a last set of recommendations—Rob of the outside, Louise of the inside—before they carried their last few items up the hill and strapped them to the luggage rack of their old Toyota. Wiping away a tear or two and waving, they slowly drove off. We watched the bouncing car disappear among the trees. We were alone!

The place felt empty, suddenly, without the Morrows. I tiptoed around on the freshly waxed wooden floors, barely daring to touch the dishes in the sink, and telling myself how Louise had left instructions to use only the special, biodegradable soap and to neatly hang the towels on the clothesline stretched between the two birch trees. I reminded Tom how Rob had said to put more wood chips on the paths around the cabins. Somehow, the harmony that prevailed in, and around, the cabins seemed to guarantee the harmony of nature as well. To tamper with one would inevitably bring about the ruin of the other. Rob's and Louise's shadows loomed large, and their names remained attached to promises of authentic wilderness experiences and union with a pristine nature.

Home Alone at the Cabin

O<small>N THE THIRD DAY OF BLISS,</small> Tom decided to drive to the nearest town, twenty or so miles away, to replenish our stock of groceries. I was reluctant to sacrifice a sunny day to be on the road, and in spite of being terrified at the idea, got up my courage to stay behind by myself with Jo, our faithful old cat. Defiantly, I declared that I would be able to "keep a lid on things" until Tom's return from his expedition.

Tom left, proudly sporting his dark brown fedora, buffalo plaid shirt, and work boots, while I treated myself to a midmorning cup of coffee. The cat had already found her spot on the porch and was curled up on the cot, purring quietly and enjoying the warmth of the sunlight on her summer fur. I was sipping coffee from one of the six white porcelain mugs left by Rob and Louise that each bore on the side a different kind of wild bird. Did I want the mallard or the Canada goose? In accord with my mood, I chose the pheasant.

I was sitting quietly at the desk on the front porch, leafing through several books about the area left by Rob and Louise: *Canoeing the Western Boundary Waters, The Story of the Sioux, The Chippewas, The History of the Voyageurs, Early Settlers in the Arrowhead Region.*

Reconnected with the stories of my childhood, I enjoyed the sun and the breeze, and listened to the soft music of the Japanese wind chimes hanging from the porch ceiling. I surveyed the extent of the new turf in front of me. Beyond the bird feeder, a large field stretched all the way to a line of tall and slender aspen mixed with spruces and occasional clumps of jack and red pines. To the right, the Vermilion flowed swiftly. Rob had informed us that the previous year, a voyageur's cup had been retrieved intact from the riverbed.

While I was musing on the history of the place, I noticed a black spot in the distance. Absorbed in my thoughts, I registered it without consciously reflecting on it. It grew larger and took on the shape of a young dog, and then it grew larger still. All of a sudden I realized this was no dog—no, it was a bear! It was ambling across the field, straight in the direction of our cabin, and it was getting bigger with every step it took. Tom was miles away. And there was no car, which meant I had no way of escaping. These thoughts raced through my head as I looked sideways at the sleeping cat. "You are no good, Jo," I muttered. "You don't even earn your keep. What are you doing to defend me?"

By now the shape was clearly visible with all its markings: the rounded ears, the pointed snout; I even thought I could see the deep-seated dark eyes. Bears are harmless unless provoked, echoed Rob's words in my head. Recent newspaper articles about a couple of mauled campers seemed to contradict his reassuring words. In vain, I rummaged around in search of the bear whistle. In my panic I remembered that the night before Tom had mentioned there was an old shotgun under the bed, as well as a few shells in the chest of drawers. I ran to the bedroom, grabbed the gun, pawed through the drawers, found the shells, and, with a shaking hand, proceeded to insert one into the chamber that I had managed to snap open. Which end went in first? The metal or cardboard? I tried one way, and it seemed to fit. I rushed back out to the porch with my loaded gun, cursing the cat again for not being a dog and realizing that I could not simply shoot through the screen. I opened the door and stepped outside, where I found myself practically nose to nose with a good-sized adult black bear. I fumbled with the shotgun. How was I supposed to hold it? The adventure tales of Karl May flashed through my mind. Finally, my childhood readings could be put to the test. I held the gun up to my right shoulder, aimed upward, and pulled the trigger. *Bam!* The sound roared through the air and echoed against the line of trees. The recoil knocked me to the ground. While tumbling I just had time to see the bear's big rump. It had spun around and was now careening away at top speed with its hind feet tucked under it and touching down well ahead of its front paws. I sat up straight. Now that the confrontation was over, I suddenly felt pretty good. Ha, I said to myself. I did it. I survived my first encounter with a bear.

At that very moment Tom came running down the hill. "Are you all right?" he shouted from afar. "What's happening?" He had heard the gunshot as he was unloading his case of Huber beer from the truck and, expecting the worst, bolted down the path toward the cabin. He was relieved to find me in fine form and beaming. After hearing my story, he declared that he felt mighty proud of his gun moll. "You did good, you did good," he joked and looked at me approvingly. I was lapping up the compliments and we walked around all day feeling a special bond. I felt I had become truly initiated into life in the wilderness.

Afterward, when we had become accustomed to living with our various "neighbors," we would often laugh when reminiscing about my fear on that first day.

Summer Pleasures

−12− W ARM WEATHER MIXED WITH RAINS made the ashes and aspens look lush green that summer. Flowering bushes covered the landscape with pink and white splotches; the birds sang all morning long. It was an intense period of renewal that relegated to oblivion lingering memories of stress and city life. We tried to emulate Rob and Louise by keeping the cabins looking as if they were fashioned after photographs in *Country Living*. To sustain the illusion, I put out some bright red geraniums; Tom's efforts to be faithful to Rob's legacy consisted in caring for our "lawn," that is, the small rectangle in front of the cabin where the grass had been kept short and free of saplings.

To instill a little order in the wilderness, Tom used the large machine he had inherited from Rob, including the habit of referring to it by its brand name, the "Jari." Somehow the word had a special resonance each time he pronounced it. The bond between man and machine was immediately transferred from one owner to the next. From the very start, Tom and his Jari formed a happy couple. The big blue machine had a rakelike extension with two rows of metal teeth that worked like sickles to cut anything in their path, from grass to weeds to saplings and small trees. Once the motor was turned on, the machine moved on its own. The operator was not so much pushing it as guiding or directing it in its unstoppable march forward. Over the years, Tom and his Jari became inseparable. In a moderately wet summer, the Jari came out of its hiding place in the shed every two weeks or so, and the mowing ceremony could begin anew.

From inside the cabin, I could see them approach. Tom, in his blue overalls, matching blue cap with an American flag, and tall workman's boots with reinforced steel toes, steered the heavy machine around the uneven terrain. Like any other partner, the Jari had its moments of unpredictability. It abruptly accelerated or, at other times, stopped. From time to time Tom paused and wiped his face with a red-and-white bandana to keep the flies off.

Even when the two disappeared from view, I could hear the motor. Together, man and machine moved forward with a deafening racket that alarmed everything that could move. Frogs fled in front of the sicklebar, their legs stretched out horizontally behind them; bugs jumped, birds fluttered in bewilderment, hapless toads waddled along to escape the deadly reaper. Unperturbed, Tom and his Jari moved ahead. In their wake lay a desolate field of grasses, stubs of aspen, violets, and blue cornflowers. Careful to avoid slaughtering animals and sparing patches of daisies, Tom was smiling mysteriously; he had entered into a world foreign to me. Rob had passed on the secret and opened a new universe. After going around and around the cabin in narrow circles like a couple of birds of prey, the happy duo finally surged up the path and disappeared into the woods. I could hear them moving through the trees for a long time before the noise finally faded in the distance.

Tom took special pride in the dirt road that led from the county road to the parking knoll. When the grass is cut, the path, with the overhanging aspens and maples, looks like a Vermont road, declared Tom, echoing Rob and Louise. Perhaps the Vermont road looks like one in the North Woods, I retorted tartly. Tom gave me a long, disapproving look. He liked his forest road and focused his efforts on grooming it. After a couple of hours, Tom and Jari reappeared, still chugging and chopping along as loudly as before. Occasionally the motor faltered, but otherwise the machine showed no sign of slowing down. Its partner, on the other hand, had a haggard look—the sweaty, dirty face, lips thin with effort. The eyes, however, were glistening, and happiness somehow radiated from behind the fatigue. I wondered what the secret of this union was that continued to elude me. I would never know.

The ritual with Jari was often followed by a canoe trip to the nearby falls, where cares and worries quickly vaporized in the rainbow-colored mist. How I loved gliding down the smooth waters on which the tall trees and pink clouds were casting their reflections and from which an early-evening mist was already rising. In our first years, complete silence was underlined by the rhythmic sound of the paddles, the hum of insects, and the cries of eagles or ravens, at times even by that of the northern loon.

Other times, we opted for a dip in the river. Our "swimming hole," off the big boulder we visited on the very first day, must have been the designated spot at least since the time of the homesteaders. Over the years, we would surprise—and in turn be surprised by— much wildlife at that spot. Bears, ferrets, and deer would appear out of nowhere. Once, a giant buck with huge antlers ran right by us, jumped into the river, and swam across. Another time, a couple of year-old bears, still wet from the river, stood on the rock and gave us a mischievous look. The area was also full of toads and frogs, especially in midsummer; we had to tread with care to give them time to seek shelter. The reddish rock, shaped like a terrace, must have served as a lookout or as a resting area for animals and humans for centuries.

We used the trunk of a dead ash tree hanging over the water for lowering ourselves into and lifting ourselves out of the river. We knew that, once we were in the water, we had to start paddling right away to fight the swift current, while navigating to avoid the boulders. Tom always swam with his goggles on. He liked to explore the underworld and excitedly reported seeing a big bass, small pike, a school of walleye, turtles, deer carcasses, an array of lost lures, a choice of beer cans, and, occasionally, even algae. Temperatures permitting, he swam a good mile or so, oblivious to the world above water. Once, two mellow older folks outfitted with pith helmets drifted by in their canoe and courteously greeted him, perhaps a bit surprised upon encountering a freestyler with goggles in the middle of a "wilderness" river. Tom kept his calibrated upstream pace. His head alternately turning left and right while counting, he never so much as acknowledged their presence.

While Tom was exploring the mysteries of the world below, I took in the sights and sounds above, from the swift-moving water sparkling in the brilliant sunlight to the colors of the rustling trees and flocks of birds. The countryside looked different from the water. The taller cattails and what I learned was wild rice growing in front of them swayed in the breeze. Red-winged blackbirds fluttered between the tall shafts of the reeds, and their shrill song filled the air. A few frightened ducks flew out of the reeds and raced ahead of us as we made our way upstream. A group of swallows sat on the branches of a dead oak farther up.

It took me some time to muster enough courage to swim past what turned out to be a sizable beaver lodge at the foot of the promontory on which our lower cabin stood. The animals were constantly fixing up their house as I could tell from the presence of fresh green twigs on top of the wooden structure. I loved watching the cute little critters swim about in the evening hours. Yet, I decided early on to avoid an encounter and never entered the water before seven in the morning or after seven in the evening.

I had to swim vigorously, both to beat the current and to keep warm. I heard ravens croaking in the distance and a squirrel chatter with indignation. We reached the end of our field, where an old tree trunk served as a sunning place for painted turtles. As I approached, six of them, of various sizes, were on the lookout. Their necks were stretched out, their heads at an obtuse angle to their shells. The yellow stripes on the sides of their necks and their red color below were a reassuring sign that they were not snappers. I tried to swim by them as quietly as possible in order not to disturb them. The smallest hopped into the river first, then the medium-sized ones plopped in the water in unison. The large veterans held out the longest. It seemed to be their way of saying, We know what this is all about. Finally, though, just before I reached them, they, too, left their spot in the sun. When, half an hour later, we passed by again on our way downstream, the turtles had already climbed back up onto the rock, and again not quite trusting us, one by one repeated the same maneuver.

Occasionally, the eagle swooped down from his dying white pine high on a nearby cliff to check us out. The first time this happened, my heart skipped several beats. I was swimming a few yards from Tom when I saw the eagle flying down the middle of the river toward us. At first, while he was still up in the air, his approach did not seem menacing. But he grew considerably in size as he lowered his altitude, until his wingspan (six feet for an adult bird, according to my book) could be verified empirically from my somewhat helpless position in the water. "Tom," I screamed, "the eagle!" Unperturbed by the approaching predator, Tom calmly pursued his freestyle. "Tom!" I bellowed in one more desperate attempt. No answer. I gave up. I turned around and started kicking up water so as to repel the eagle, which, I thought, would not be able to mistake me for a duckling.

Either the eagle had approached simply out of curiosity, or he was convinced by my method of self-defense. In either case, he reversed his course and soared back up into the air, higher and higher, until his size had shrunk to a large black dot again. I could see him circling first over the water, then over the field until he disappeared from sight behind the trees. After this incident, about which I was soon able to laugh, the eagle returned several times more. I now began to imagine that he was coming to greet me. He always met me at the same point, toward the end of the field. He lowered himself, took a good look and then, with a majestic sweep of his wings, prepared to circle back up, high into the sky.

Forest Paths

AFTER OUR FORAYS AROUND THE CABIN, as well as on and in the river, we were more than eager to begin exploring the rest of our surroundings, so we decided to blaze a trail through the forest. We set out from the lower cabin and made our way across the roughly sixty square feet of Tom's "lawn." We walked by the three weeping willows, nostalgic signs of domesticity from the homesteading era, before we ambled down the gently sloping meadow that, in early August, was covered with the first goldenrod as well as myriad asters that shone in white and purple hues. We strolled by the red and white pines that Rob had so meticulously planted in a straight row along the river. The trees were intended to serve as windscreens and antierosion devices, and also to discourage the beaver population, which does not care for coniferous trees, from expanding. How we longed to see them grow (and how we wished they hadn't, a few years later, when they completely obstructed our view). That day, we stopped at the highest point of the field, from which we had a rare glimpse of the countryside in all four directions. Before us, the river stretched majestically from south to north. We surveyed the wide bend to the south, the swampy part with a defunct duck blind from another age, and the straight part directly in front of us where the opposite shores were covered by the crests of tall pine trees. The river gradually narrowed at the rapids toward the north end of our land. It had carved out a little gorge and then turned to the left before disappearing from sight. "This place is ours!" Too good to be true, wasn't that the saying? We sighed, with a mixture of both pleasure and uneasy anticipation.

Continuing our journey through the tall grass, where wild lilies were blooming, we reached the point of entry into the woods. Following the narrow path that had most likely been marked out several centuries earlier, we entered the forest and stopped to look up at the aspen trees whose crowns were moving back and forth. They were mixed with the more rigid spruces and some scrubby balsam firs.

A thick layer of moss, leaves, and pine needles absorbed the sound of our footsteps. The cries of birds pierced the silence, though already there were fewer than in early summer. The shrill sounds of the blue jays and the deeper cries of the gray Canadian jays—also known as whiskey jacks—seemed defiant. The chickadees' cheery notes were a constant presence and comfort. After a while, the winding path narrowed, and Tom used his axe on brush and overhanging branches. He was thrilled when he spotted rings of mushrooms along the way. He crouched on several occasions to pick a specimen that he then sniffed while intoning its Latin names and general classification. I patiently endured the lectures but also abandoned myself to the hum of the late-summer forest and the rustling of the leaves.

We had already crossed a small creek and were now arriving at its main fork. The translucent water sparkled in the sun as it flowed over boulders left behind by a receding glacier. A few hand-hewn logs laid across the creek served as a bridge. "How quaint!" I exclaimed. Tom wanted to follow the creek to the river, so we turned instead of crossing the bridge and walked alongside the stream, stumbling over fallen logs, dodging overhanging hazelnut branches, and trying to stay clear of the spiny hawthorns while admiring the bright red bunchberries and palmlike ferns. We pushed on through the thick brush, skirted a grove of white pine, and arrived at the rivulet's confluence with an even smaller creek. The faint sound of the wind, the fast-moving, clear waters, and the blue sky made us feel that the vision of peace and harmony had become a reality.

We were feeling almost ecstatic when we spotted a couple of trees whose bark seemed to have been shaved off about two feet or so above the ground. The bare trunks were sculpted into a distinct hourglass shape that signaled—I remembered distantly from Walt Disney movies and more immediately from the weathered stumps I had seen in our balsam grove—the presence of beavers. "Beaver ho!" I joked. We laughed and regretted only not seeing any of these cute little critters swimming around. We had no way of knowing that this was not only the first, but also the last, time we would see the rivulet flowing freely. We were embarking on a prolonged adventure. That day, feeling our souls expanding in what looked like untouched nature, and quickly forgetting about the beavers, we simply continued our first journey in the woods, across a tributary and over the next hill until we reached the Vermilion River.

The Art of Ricing

THE SMALL NORTH WOODS COMMUNITIES still followed the seasons. In addition to national and family holidays, the fishing opener, blueberry season, the wild rice harvest, and various hunting seasons punctuated the year. Late August or early September was the time for harvesting the wild rice that grew in lakes and rivers. For more than a century now, ricing had been reserved for Native Americans, who often harvested it to sell. Lately, commercial paddy growers in California had so deflated the market that harvesting rice manually was no longer profitable. But the ritual survived, and many still took pleasure in it—and also, as we would soon find out, a modicum of pain.

We had discovered that, along our stretch of the Vermilion, a narrow bed of rice was growing that expanded into a wide area at the southern bend of the river. We watched over the ripening of the delicate stalks and impatiently looked forward to the opening day. Not that we were experts in ricing. Several times a year, we cooked wild rice bought at the supermarket for special guests; Tom had told me in emphatic and poetic terms about how it was harvested by Native Americans pushing their canoes through the shallow waters of the rice beds. I perked up. Like most Europeans of my generation, I retained a respectful fascination for anything related to Native American culture and was keen to find out more about its customs. I visualized svelte and muscular bodies with long jet-black hair gliding silently over the waters and was eager to witness the scene.

A few years before we bought our cabins, we had canoed the river farther up, at its wide part above the falls; there I had seen rice beds for the first time. Wild rice looked somewhat like wheat growing in shallow waters. The stalks were still green and blended in with reeds, shrubs, ash trees, and other vegetation along the shore. When we spotted the rice, we thought we had discovered a private cache and vowed to return during the season. Ricing in Minnesota, I learned, was strictly regulated by the Department of Natural Resources. One had to get a license and set out on a certain day, at an assigned time. Only after the first week, and once all the rice had been harvested, was there unrestricted access to the lakes and rivers.

Following the rules, we returned on a crisp and clear Saturday afternoon in early September to rice in our secret place. We parked the car on a gravel road, put the canoe into a shallow creek, and painfully poled more than paddled our way through thick reeds and mud in the direction of the river. The goal was to reach the open part of the river where we had seen the bed. When we emerged from the reeds into the wider part of the river, the rice was bright yellow and stood out against the dark low line of black spruces that separated them from the intense blue of the boreal sky. The wind gusting from the north made dark swirls on the water. The brilliance of the light contrasted sharply with the starkness of the landscape. We heard only the rustling of leaves and the distant thunder of the waterfall that separated this lakelike part of the river from the lower rapids. The guttural croak of a raven could be heard in the distance. A beaver swam out from his "Marriott" along the shore. Indignant at our invasion of his territory, he circled the canoe and then disappeared after slapping his tail in protest.

We lost ourselves in contemplation for a few minutes before Tom suggested that we paddle over to the rice beds. Surprise! Almost all the rice was gone. After a bit, we began to laugh, timidly at first, but soon we were roaring. How could we have been so naive as to believe for even one moment that we were the only ones to know about this place? Our stash was not so private after all, and neither were the North Woods. Instead of conceding defeat, however, we decided to try our luck anyway.

Although we had our license, neither of us knew how to harvest the grains. Tom had heard of sticks being used to beat the seeds into the canoe and had come prepared with a fallen branch. I had only my bare hands. Our daughter, home from college for a few days, was sitting in the bottom of the canoe, lost in the mysterious world of Doris Lessing. In the meantime, her parents poked through the reeds and picked a few remaining grains of rice here and there. The rice heads, I noticed, were brownish yellow; the husks were long and could be opened by hand to expose the green seeds, which were hard and tasted like flour. We spent some time paddling around, gathering a few more grains and laughing at our fiasco while still caught in the spell of the intense beauty of this early-fall afternoon.

After what seemed like a lot of hard work, we finally went home with a couple of pounds of rice. Later, we spread it out to dry on a piece of cloth. We waited patiently, but for some reason, the grain never seemed to change color or begin to even faintly resemble the kind we bought at the supermarket. We even tried to cook some, but it remained hard and inedible. Only later did we find out that an involved process was necessary to prepare the rice for cooking. It had to be parched and kilned, and the husks had to be loosened from the seeds. The green seeds turned dark brown in the heat of the operation. Then they were separated into grades. There was, indeed, so much to discover in the North Woods.

Having learned our lesson from the earlier failed outing, we decided as proud new cabin owners that this year, we would rice in front of our own place. Here, at long last, nobody could take it away from us. For the past weeks, we had been scrupulously following the maturation of the precious plants. It was a drought year, but the unrelenting intensity of the sun had produced kernels that seemed larger than the ones we had seen before. Two days before the harvest date, a storm swept through the area. Torrential rains beat down on the stalks, and the river swelled to new heights to submerge the few remaining upright ones. Through the sheets of water pouring from the cabin roof and gushing down along Rob's Japanese rain chain, we watched our crop float down the river and sighed. Reluctantly, we decided to follow the advice of friends and go to a neighboring lake known for its extensive rice beds; there we would compete with other ricers.

We rose early on the appointed day. Unperturbed by streaming rain but now better informed as to the techniques of ricing, we collected our sticks, still called batons from the days of the voyageurs, with which we would knock the rice off the stalks into the canoe. The season opened at nine in the morning, but we had been told that ricers would be lined up, ready to put in their canoes. As we drove south, the rains suddenly stopped. Everything was still dripping by the time we reached the parking lot near the lake, but the sun burst through the clouds. In spite of the early hour, people were bustling about in colorful jackets and ponchos, unloading canoes from their cars and pickups. Precisely at nine, the self-important official from the Department of Natural Resources would blow his whistle and people would hurry their canoes into the water.

A motley crowd was assembled. It consisted of oddly dressed and bearded characters in jalopies; some were greenhorns like ourselves, eager to experience the ritual. Several Native Americans, lithe and intense, were first in line. We, of course, were close to last. But this time we were fully outfitted. We were equipped with batons, a burlap bag for our booty, and a license. When our turn came, we headed out into the lake in our tippy red fiberglass canoe. I was in the front but sat aftward, ready to beat the rice into the canoe. Tom was manning the stern, guiding the canoe slowly and steadily through the rice beds.

The object of the game was to make long straight lines across the lake, from one shore to the other. One person paddled while the other bent the stalks over the gunwales of the canoe and beat them to knock the kernels into the boat. Ricing turned out to be backbreaking. I mustered all my strength and tried not to show signs of fatigue. Tom, the more enduring of us, was steadily and patiently paddling away. The bottom of the canoe was slowly filling with rice kernels. Once the first layer was in, the kernels took on a fuzzy look. This meant that they were beginning to accumulate. Not without horror and disgust, I noticed worms crawling in all directions while armies of spiders tried to climb up the sides of the canoe, mostly unsuccessfully. Nature was indeed teeming with life. I had the fleeting impression that, perhaps, the purity, peace, and harmony I was looking for in nature existed mainly in the abstract. The rice came with worms, spiders, and other bugs.

For the time being, however, we were smoothly gliding along.

The silence of the day was punctuated by the rhythmic swishing of the batons hitting the rice and the paddle dipping into the water. The canoes had dispersed, and in the distance we could occasionally see a shadow, the silhouette of a Chippewa gliding through the reeds. Whereas we were both sitting down, in their canoes the person steering stood in the rear and used a long pole to push against the bottom of the lake. (A paddle, it seemed, was only a hindrance.)

Without being able to rival them, Tom and I worked, so we told each other, with great efficiency. In the meantime, the low rain clouds had all lifted and were soon burned off by a radiant September sun. Rice lakes tend to have low shorelines, and this one was no exception. It too was bordered by thin, tall black spruces, the telltale sign of the north. I was soon lost in reverie, warming up in the sun and absorbed into the brilliance of the early-fall colors, the yellow of the rice, the dark line of trees, and the dark blue sky. A few birds flew overhead. First a heron with his long legs stretched out behind him, then a kingfisher with his crest ruffled, lending him a gruff look. Tom grew disenchanted with my casual way of ricing and proposed switching places. I readily agreed and took up the seat in the back of the canoe.

I let myself be drawn into the sensations of nature while Tom was steadily harvested the rice. After a couple of hours of paddling, sitting on the hard bench, my arms were getting tired and my back muscles began to protest. I insisted on lunch. Breaking for lunch was certainly unusual for ricers, who followed the laws of the market, that is, of the relation between the least amount of time out and the greatest amount harvested. Not without grumbling, Tom agreed to stop, and we chose a boulder on the shore from which we could survey the entire lake. In the distance, we could see only a few heads moving about: ricers were now spread out over the vast surface. Tom popped a cheap bottle of French red wine. We concocted sandwiches with French cheese and Dijon mustard and forgot about the competition.

We did make it back into the water for another hour or so. Then we noticed that the official time was up and we began the strenu- ous trip back. We proudly arrived on shore with what looked like a good cargo. Our pride vanished when we looked at the canoes of our Chippewa neighbors. They had double and even triple our amount! Somewhat crestfallen, we headed back to our cabin, laughing about our clumsiness in maneuvering our craft and in harvesting the rice, but also with a feeling of pride at having made it through the day.

Winter Pleasures

THAT YEAR, FROM THANKSGIVING ON, the snow accumulated, and we discovered the North Woods anew on skis. With the leaves fallen from the trees, and the lower brush covered with snow, the open forest offered new vistas. We became avid skiers and indulged in our new sport whenever we could.

We developed the habit of setting out shortly after a copious breakfast. More so than other meals at the cabin, the breakfast ritual had a special flavor that was enhanced in the winter. It began when Tom rose from the hand-hewn log bed left us by Rob and Louise. He disappeared into the main part of the cabin to revive the fire in the cast-iron woodstove. Tucked into my red flannel sheets and covered by an oversized down comforter, with my ears I followed his progress from the pattern of familiar noises. I listened to the coffee beans being ground in a hand-cranked iron mill before the clank of the percolator said it was being put on the stove. Then there was the clatter of dishes and silverware taken from the metal drawers by the sink and placed on the wooden table. When the percolator was bubbling heavily, I judged that the moment to get up had come. Nothing ever tasted like the freshly brewed coffee with soft-boiled eggs, toast, and the jam that over the years would evoke smells and images of later summer days, of pine trees on the secret blueberry hill we discovered just beyond our land and of tall, lush field grasses among which the raspberry bushes grew in the midst of stumps left by beavers who had worked the forest at the edge of the field. Energized, we could then plan the day.

By the time we had washed the dishes in snow water heated on the stove and dried them with Louise's waffle towels, the rays of the sun were already filtering through some lingering clouds, and the landscape was scintillating in a golden orange hue in which a few snowflakes were still dancing. We hurried to get ready. Since I tended to be a bit on the chilly side, I outfitted myself in an over-sized classic, "camospeckled" blaze orange hunter's outfit—"très chic," one of my French friends, ignorant of American hunters' customs, was later to remark upon seeing me pictured in this garb. Tom was more stylishly dressed in a tight, sleeveless vest and long woolen socks that made him look as if he were wearing knickers. —27—

After waxing our skis with what Tom, based on mysterious calculations, judged to be the proper color, we set forth. Tom performed what in guidebooks is referred to as "blazing the trail." In his case, this largely meant that he sank into the snow up to his knees and, in spite of the freshly waxed skis, stomped, huffed, and puffed, very unlike what one sees in the videos teaching cross-country skiing or advertising winter pleasures in the North Woods. I had the easier task as the rear guard. Shaking with laughter, I took a perverse pleasure in watching his dubious progress.

From the cabin we cut a trail across the immaculate white field and followed the river up to the edge of the forest. When we looked back, we could see the little cabin in the distance with its snow-covered roof and the plume of smoke coming out of its tall chimney. My vision had come true. How cute, I exclaimed once more, while Tom muttered something about polluting the atmosphere. The sparkling landscape against the blue sky and the intense winter sun, the moisture in the air that made the atmosphere glisten, both invigorated and exhilarated. The snow and the cold hushed and heightened the sounds at the same time. A few ice crystals flickered in the lingering morning mist. We skied toward the far end of the field, where we joined the forest path.

This part of the path was usually prepared for us by hunters who came to this area every year in November and who drove their four-wheelers or snowmobiles through the forest to set up their stands on adjacent county land. They cleared the way in exchange for being allowed to bring their machines onto our land. Like feudal landlords, we put up with their yearly passage because out of it we got a partially groomed trail for skiing. Sunlight filtered through the upper canopy, casting oblique rays and giving the forest an air of mystery. The trees kept the wind out, and we felt the warmth of the sun as we glided along the light-filled path in the new powder. The winding path, packed down by the hunters, provided, at last, some effortless skiing up and down the gently rolling landscape. We crossed several small ridges. In their valleys, little creeks leading down to the river were now frozen solid to the point that we did not give the earlier beaver shavings much thought. We did conclude from the number and variety of tracks that we shared our trail with numerous animals. In fact, in many areas the trail looked like a deer highway.

We were beginning to read tracks, just like the characters in my childhood stories, though we were still in the early stages and couldn't identify all of them. The most impressive ones, in addition to the deep imprints of the moose, were those of a lone wolf that had followed the trail at most an hour or so earlier, judging from the clear outline of the prints and the droppings, which Tom examined with great seriousness, the way we had been instructed to do in our Audubon book. I made a brave effort to participate in the handling and sniffing of the scat.

At one point the path divided. If we kept going straight in the direction of federal land and the Boundary Waters, we would leave our forest at the foot of the pine-covered hill where we picked blueberries. We dubbed it "Blueberry Hill" in honor of Fats Domino. We never tired of singing our favorite line about "finding our thrill on Blueberry Hill." The view from the top was indeed breath-taking: a seemingly endless forest stretched below well beyond the horizon, modulated into parallel ridges covered with thick forest and traversed by the winding river. Over the years, Blueberry Hill would become one of our favorite lookouts and points of excursion. Today we opted for the better ski trail and turned onto county land. The trail, groomed by the hunters, led into the old part of the forest up a medium-sized hill dotted with large boulders.

Eventually we arrived at the point where the snowmobile trail ended in a loop and our prefabricated path came to an end. From then on we were on our own. After climbing over some fallen logs and ducking under large, overhanging spruce branches, we reached a clearing—the remains of a huge beaver pond. It took us quite a while to realize that this was the very creek that, farther down, ran through our own forest and along which, during the summer, we had first sighted a few "beaver trees." I mused over how far up beavers swam from the river in search of a quiet area where they could set up shop and build a lodge. I had recently heard that only "lazy beavers"—the virtues of hard work extended even to the beaver world—built their mansions, like the one in front of our cabin, on the river. Others, more virtuous, selected a creek that they then proceeded to dam up below their lodge in order to make a lake in which they could swim happily ever after.

Nature lovers praised the beavers' "built" environment by saying that it created habitat for deer, frogs, fish, birds, and other wildlife. At the same time, I declared after surveying this old beaver clearing that it made a mess and killed all the trees. The trees that were spared by the beavers' long sharp teeth—which they had to use continuously in gnawing wood to prevent them from growing longer—suffocated in the muddy waters. Once an area had been depleted of resources, the beavers moved upstream or downstream. This is how the inside "valleys" between the gently sloping ridges leading down to the river all became filled over time with beaver ponds. Some ponds were active and some were defunct.

The one we were contemplating from the edge of the forest was defunct and had been for some time. Old beaver ponds were supposedly fertile ground and, after a lengthy cycle, would once again be covered with lush plants and trees. Now, however, it was an open expanse with a few stumps that, like war victims, were hopelessly and silently reaching toward the sky, and with many dead trees lying around helter-skelter. The latter were covered with snow and would make the crossing treacherous, since visibility was reduced and one could easily fall into a hole. It gave the area an eerie look. It smacked of cheap nature art, of pieces of wood that were sold in local souvenir shops as sculptures.

Beaver ponds were passable only in the winter months when they were frozen. Like lazy beavers, I opted for the easy way out and was in favor of turning around and following the groomed path. Tom, who liked difficulties, was in favor of forging ahead. And so he did, without much hesitation or even a look back. Since I did not want to be stranded in the forest with the wolves, I trailed along, still muttering and soon swearing after my first good tumble head first into the deep snow. What looked like a log, under the snow, had proved hollow. After a few more falls accompanied by strong expletives, we paused in the middle of the pond, huffing and puffing, and with my declaring that no one would even faintly consider this to be cross-country skiing.

All was perfectly still. The winter sun was rendered more intense by the reflection of the snow. We looked around at the tall aspen forest we had just left and at the dark spruces toward which we were heading. Tom pulled out a flask of bourbon; we removed our skis and sat down on a fallen log. Drunk with sunlight and the brilliance of the countryside as much as with our sips of bourbon, we bubbled in harmony with the wintry landscape.

Now in a jolly mood and with flushed cheeks, no longer feeling the occasional pain after a tumble, we continued our trek until we reached the thick spruce forest on the opposite side of the pond. We found another trail made by hunters on snowmobiles and followed it over several other steep hills that gave us plenty of opportunities to "schuss down" on the other side. The show usually ended in several more tumbles that, especially with help of the bourbon, provided the person who hadn't fallen with a good laugh and with increasingly elaborate accounts to tell about the other's demise. After another mile or two, the path led over what, from a distance, looked like another "ridge" but turned out to be the outer wall of a huge, ten-foot-tall beaver dam that separated the higher and, so we discovered, active pond from the lower, abandoned one. Behind the dam, the beaver house looked very well kept.

On the other side of the dam, a second pond looked even larger than the first. It covered at least twenty acres. As we glided along the path around the pond, we found large stands of aspens whose trunks had been gnawed at, three feet above the snow cover. So this was what an "active" beaver area looked like. I could imagine the little beavers coming out at night to find their trees. They would stand up against them and chew away at the bark to their heart's content, that is, until they had eaten their fill, grooming and grinding their teeth in the process.

How did the beavers get out of their lodge since their entrance was under water? Tom, who seemed more knowledgeable about beavers, explained that they made tunnels from under the water up into the lakeshore or the riverbanks that enabled them to emerge in the open. The openings were in the ground, not just in the ice. Beavers, he repeated, were nature's engineers. They sure were. Yet, looking at the results, I began to feel some ambivalence. All the tree trunks we saw had a characteristic hourglass indentation. Some were far along and ready to topple over. Others barely had the trace of a nibble. Shavings were lying around everywhere. What would the beavers do with the trees? In fall they stashed the leaves away for food on cold winter days. Part of the wood was used for the upkeep of their house. In the winter they most likely did not do much with it, but tried to keep their teeth ground. The fallen logs also helped animals move, especially in winter. They could run along on them, above the deep snow. Not that beavers actually run. Because they are aquatic mammals, they have webbed hind feet and on land maneuver only slowly and with difficulty. Their habitat is the water, but they can manage in the snow. They construct veritable slides that enable them to move more freely. We saw some troughs in the snow that looked deep and wide—like bathtubs, I joked.

It was hard not to like the beavers, even if they did create havoc. In addition to the aspens, some of the birches and ash trees showed incisions as well, though they were clearly second choice on the beavers' menu. Their bark was harder and chewier for the discriminating palate of the beavers, who preferred the softer bark of the aspen. And with successive loggings and little replanting, more and more aspens were growing at this point. It was beavers' paradise! Not only had they made a comeback, there were more beavers now than in the eighteenth century. Somehow, somewhere, the sight of the vast beaver pond had touched a nerve. It had made a chink in my blissful feeling of harmony.

Beavers have few natural enemies. Their pelts had lost all value when animal rightists began to militate against wearing fur. What would be the fate of the expanding population? Landowners all over the North Woods, we would soon learn, were surreptitiously killing the beavers who were felling their cherished trees. Until now, we had protested such inhuman conduct over territorial disputes. Little did we know that this was only the beginning of our own encounter with *Castor canadensis.*

Leaving the beaver pond behind, we headed back into the tall aspen forest, and after a steady climb, arrived at an open field from which we could look over the entire area. Miles and miles of forest stretched out in front of us. We were overwhelmed by the silence. The faint sound of the wind whistling in the trees was interspersed with the occasional crack of a branch and the flutter of wings. From there on, we were on easy street, gently gliding downhill through the powder snow. We came across the early settlers' old "potato field" that was now used by hunters, past the old hermit's cabin, the former site of the sawmill, and back out into the field that had been made tillable by homesteaders through backbreaking effort. It struck me that we, and the Morrows before us, were now trying just as hard to replant trees for a wilderness effect.

We finished our "loop" by crossing the field and soon were back at the cabin. By then the wind had died down, and it was warm enough to sit outside in Rob and Louise's flowered plastic lawn chairs—future antiques—and have some well-deserved, home-cooked barley soup. We sat enjoying the food and basking in the sun, while looking south, up the frozen river and along the ridges on stood tall aspen and pine trees, survivors of successive loggings by beavers and humans.

Of Mice and Men

THAT EVENING, PLEASANTLY TIRED FROM OUR SKIING, we retired early. In the beginning, I found the quiet at night eerie. Tom was a sound sleeper, but I would wake up and hear all the unfamiliar noises. In the city there were sirens and airplanes taking off and landing, accelerating and decelerating on the flight path directly over our house. I was used to the incessant rumble, the tension, and the so-called nerve-racking pace of urban life. But in the North Woods, at first I was disquieted by the uncanny sounds of nature. I lay awake listening, not without anguish, to the slurping noises from the river. What kinds of critters were rummaging around in the moonlight? There were howls off in the distance, sometimes a squeal. What dramas were being played out? Occasionally, the noises made our old cat, Jo, stir, but mostly she pretended to ignore them and remained solidly entrenched in the fluffy down comforter. Toward morning there were even louder noises coming from underneath the cabin. Something was playing soccer with the empty cans and washbasins that were stored there. Something else was jumping onto the roof from nearby branches. There would be a thud, then a moment of silence, followed by the pitter-patter of little feet running over the roof. At times there were cracking noises coming from the forest. A deer? A bear? I would never know. The noises ebbed and flowed, shrouded in the mysteries of the night.

Yet for several weeks now, ever since Thanksgiving, to be precise, another strange noise had been audible, this time inside the cabin. It began with a scraping sound against metal, then quiet and some fumbling around, followed by a light thump. These noises were followed by louder, more or less continuous sounds on the wooden floor. Many times, I had tried to get out of the bed and tiptoe past the wall-divider to investigate their cause. It was to no avail. As soon as I rose, all fell silent. Then I tried again, stealthily climbing out of the old wooden bed and silently crossing the cold floor. I courageously switched on my flashlight in the direction of the noise. Nothing. I had to repeat the maneuver several times. After a while I got so good at creeping through the dark cabin that I was certain, this time, that the perpetrator of this late-night activity would not escape. I had, over the weeks, become bolder and was no longer afraid of being attacked. I stopped, held my breath, and waited for the noise to resume. There, I heard it again, right in front of me. Determined, I switched on the light and aimed it at the noise. On the floor, in front of me, a tiny gray mouse sat on its hind legs, its front paws with their tiny, delicate, pink fingers clutching a large walnut, which it was rolling across the floor to a destination unknown to me. The mouse looked up with its shiny black eyes. "What are you going to do to me?" it seemed to say. "Don't bother me while I roll my beautiful nut."

The mouse was so cute, it looked as if it had stepped out of a children's storybook. Stuart Little! I stood there motionless, enchanted by the sight of the mouse pushing its giant nut. Sisyphus was a country mouse. My inaction was interpreted positively by the mouse. It resumed its activity and arduously pushed the nut across the floor until it disappeared in a hole so tiny that I had never even noticed it.

Now I could reconstruct the scene and make sense of it all. For

Thanksgiving, we had bought some nuts, which we kept in a basket on top of the gas refrigerator. Like many old models, it had cooling coils in the back. The mouse had climbed up to the top, using the wires for support. It had somehow jockeyed the nut out of the basket, rolled it to the edge, and pushed it over. Then the mouse climbed back down to find its nut on the floor and roll it home.

I inspected the basket. It was almost empty. Several of the nuts had been emptied of their contents through a perfectly circular incision in their shells. I was so moved by the sight that I went to the pantry, took out the bag with the remaining nuts, and filled the basket again. Smiling at the thought of the mouse, I tiptoed back to bed, where Tom was still fast asleep. Softly admonishing the cat for not doing her duty, but happy about it, too, I climbed back into bed and nestled into the flannel sheets.

Later that night, and during many of the following nights, I would slip in and out of sleep, happily listening to the faint noises of nuts being dropped from the high refrigerator before being pushed by small delicate fingers across the smooth wooden floor.

Round-robin with the Weasels

BEAVERS, BEARS, AND MICE were not our only companions at the cabin. Late in summer Tom had found a dead weasel on the little path to our reluctant garden. The tiny animal, so cherished as ermine in earlier times by kings and queens, both as pet and adornment, bore no marks of violent death. It was in its summer phase, brown with a lighter belly. Our book about mammals, consulted on the occasion, informed us that weasels turned white only in the winter, and that even if transported to a warm climate, their coats would still turn white.

Our weasel tale happened a few days after we got ready for our New Year's celebration. We spent the week between Christmas and New Year's at the cabin. New Year's there was to become a ritual. It consisted of a ski, followed by a big dinner near a warm fire, topped off with a bottle of champagne. We kept the cork all year as a good luck sign. With full bellies, the warmth of the fire and that provided by the champagne, we always made it a point of stepping outside the cabin, glasses in hand, and toasting the year to come under the vastness of the northern skies, their scintillating winter constellations crisscrossed by an increasing number of satellites and the blinking lights of jetliners headed for distant lands.

This year, we were in a mood for celebrating. I had requested fish for dinner on New Year's Eve, and Tom wanted steak on New Year's Day. We arrived late in the afternoon, and, because our road was covered with deep snow, parked the car at the bottom of the hill near Mike and Lonnie's, our only neighbors. In the already dimming light, we made our way along the familiar two miles to the cabins without a flashlight. Loaded down with several bags of groceries, we sank into the snow well above our knees and took an occasional tumble, but refrained from the usual complaints, made giddy with the prospects of the pleasures to come.

As good ecologists, we had answered the bagger's routine question at the supermarket with "paper," though we now began to regret our virtuous decision. When we arrived at the cabin door, Tom pointed in silence to his ripped bag. The salmon steak had fallen out during our heroic struggle through the deep snow. I pretended to be a good sport. "It doesn't matter," I declared, cheerily. We would have omelettes tonight. They always tasted delicious when prepared on the cabin stove. And so we reassured each other by saying that tomorrow, in the daylight, we would set out to find the lost package. This was not the season for wildlife anyhow. Deer were vegetarians and bears were hibernating. We called off the search and settled in.

The following morning, not even a scrap of paper was anywhere in sight along the road, though the day was bright and no new snow had fallen. After a meticulous but unfruitful search, we resigned ourselves. We speculated a bit on what creature of the wild would have made a go for our salmon and left it at that. I decided instead to take good care of the steak that I took out of the orange cooler on the porch where, during winter, it served as a natural freezer, and put it on one of the old wooden kitchen counters so it would have time to thaw.

During the afternoon, I was sitting in the green wicker chair reading and enjoying my usual cup of coffee. As I was savoring the brew, my eyes, almost unconsciously, moved across the cabin floor. I glanced down in the space between the stove and the sink. A white shape caught my eyes. There, there it was. It was the package with the fish, leaning against the back wall. Tom had been mistaken. He had actually brought the package in, and it must have fallen off the counter unbeknownst to him.

Still holding my cup, I reached for the broom with my free hand. I turned the broom upside down and stuck the handle into the space to dislodge the package. It was somehow jammed, and I was unable to get it out right away. I tried again. After several frustrated attempts, I bent forward, but could not believe my eyes when, suddenly, I noticed that the package was gently moving to the right. By then I had put down my cup. I started to suspect foul play. The package moved again, haltingly. I tried to shift it again in the opposite direction with the broomstick, when out from behind the kitchen sink, there peeked a tiny white head with a black snout and a pair of beady dark eyes. It peeked around the corner, in bewilderment, as if to ask, "What are you doing, you mean, mean person? Why are you taking my food?" Soon, under the threat of the broom, the entire animal became visible. It was a weasel, resplendent in its regal white winter coat.

Since I had retrieved the package, the weasel could only retreat. I opened the cabin door wide and ordered it out. By now the weasel was as frantic as I—unless it was merely making fun of me. It began running around the table, disappearing and reemerging from behind the sink, the wooden kitchen counters, the sofa, the stove. The chase went on, round and round. After a few minutes I realized that there was not one, there were two—no, three weasels running madly in a circle. I first came to that conclusion from the difference in sizes that I nonetheless observed in the midst of the red-hot pursuit. "Out you go," I screamed and scolded. "You thieves, you took last night's dinner, too!" I had seen, when rescuing the package, the steak through the hole they had chewed in the paper. It wasn't the salmon, it was the steak they were now after. My steak! My indignation knew no bounds. In the midst of all the screaming and running, I could hear Tom outside. He was calling me, eager to find out about the source of so much commotion.

At long last, rather than reentering the circle for yet another round, one of the weasels, the leader it seemed, left its orbit and shot out the door, followed by the two smaller ones. I sank into one of the wicker chairs near the table, exhausted. I wiped the sweat off my brow and looked at my salvaged bounty that I felt I had snatched from bandits. Tom was laughing. We cut off the end that had been eaten by the weasel and roasted the rest of it in the old Magic Chef oven. I could have sworn it was the best-tasting steak we ever had. It was accompanied by a bottle of old French Bordeaux that Tom had brought for the occasion, and we toasted my bravura. We were happy about our good fortune, while making plenty of wishes for other adventures to come.

In the middle of the night we were startled by rumbling noises. Tom volunteered and went out into the main part of the cabin

to light an oil lamp. I decided to stay behind, secure under the flannel sheets and Swiss comforter. I swallowed some laughter as I heard Tom arguing with the weasels. "Now get out, get out, right now!" he said. I heard him smacking down the broom, and maybe the weasels were afraid of it now. As soon as they heard it, they retreated and calm descended upon the cabin, interrupted only by the occasional crackling and shifting of logs in the stove. As soon as Tom climbed back into bed, the racket resumed. Eventually, the weasels quit. Either they had found a piece of leftover steak or they got tired of the game. In any case, we drifted off into deep sleep and dreams of faraway weasels.

Icy Roads

THE LOCAL SNOWPLOW OPERATORS had offered to clear what we, faithful to the Morrows' tradition, called the Vermont road and what they irreverently referred to as the two-mile-long dirt pathway that connected us with the paved county road. "Yeah, just let us know," one of them said proudly, "and we'll do it for you. You betcha."

Thanking them, we declined. We preferred to keep the path closed to winter traffic, although I, especially, loathed hauling in the supplies that, based on our recent experience, were at risk of getting lost, and always urged Tom to "try the hill" with our heavy-duty four-wheeler. Late in February the snow had already begun to melt and we decided to go to the cabin for one last ski. We planned to leave early so as to arrive while it was still light.

As usual, we left the city late and arrived after it was pitch-black. The familiar silence set in as soon as we turned off the county road. The ground was still white, but bare spots were showing because the previous snowfall had been followed by a thaw and a melt. The headlights made the road seem navigable, and I only too eagerly acquiesced when Tom suggested that we attempt to drive up the hill to our gate. Parking the car and walking in, perhaps again painfully sinking into the remaining snow while carrying two days' worth of supplies was not appealing. It was all right with the bread, the vegetables, and the meat. But when it came to the water jugs, the beer, and the wine, the going was tough.

In the darkness and with the road lit only by the headlights, Tom put the car into four-wheel drive and we proudly began our ascent. At first everything seemed to go well. It was only when we got to the steep part, just before the road turned sharply and then flattened out, that the car balked. What looked like a smooth road had been a trail, packed down by snowmobilers who, because of the recent melt, could no longer use the adjacent trails. But the snowmobiles had packed the remaining snow in such a way that it was much higher in the middle than on the sides. The car bottomed out, the wheels spun, and we could not move. Tom revved the engine and released the accelerator. He tried again. It was no use. He put the car in reverse and tried to back up. It began sliding down the hill and then veered slightly to the right. Slowly, but inexorably, we started to slide off the road. Again, Tom revved the engine and the car took one last swerve to the right. The rear wheel slid off what we later would determine was a fallen log. Gently, the car sank into the deep snow. We were stuck.

We sat there for a while, in silence. Then I started to swear. I ran through my usual repertoire that went against the grain of Tom's gentlemanly manners. It was clear that we could do nothing further that night. We might as well start our long trek in and warm the cabin as well as ourselves by getting a fire going in the barrel stove. Valiantly and in complete silence, Tom was the first to leave the vehicle. He loaded the groceries into a Duluth pack, an oversized green knapsack essential for all wilderness and outbound adventures, and swung it onto his back. I grabbed several smaller items, and we set off through the woods in the dark. The flashlight we always made a point of having in the glove compartment was, as bad luck would have it, nowhere in sight. With only the light from the first-quarter moon, we made it to the top of the hill. In the process we found out that the snow was much deeper than it had initially appeared in the beam of the headlights. The silence of the starry night was broken by my swearing, which did not end until we were in the cabin.

Tom busied himself with the stove, while I groped for the bourbon I kept hidden for these special occasions in one of the cupboards. I liked my bourbon in the wilderness—it made me feel like a true lumberjack. Finally, with the warmth of the drink combined with that of the fire, we were able to relax and begin joking about our odyssey.

The odyssey was far from over. The following day brought ample sunshine and a subzero temperature. The instant we woke up the thought hit us that we had to get the car out. A few years earlier, when we still had our rusty fleet of unreliable Volkswagens, I had signed us up with AAA+. This plan provided for up to two hundred miles of free towing; the gold card would virtually guarantee a tow from anywhere between our house in the city and the North Woods. An additional twenty-five dollars paid over and above the annual fee bought security and peace of mind.

Fully confident, I dialed the 800-AAA-HELP number. A smooth male voice answered: "AAA, can I help you?" "You betcha," I retorted, adopting once more the local formula. I stated my problem and proudly gave my membership number, emphasizing the "gold plus," which was to give us extra protection. "Where are you located?" the voice fluted again. "In northern Minnesota, near the Vermilion River," I said.

The ensuing silence must have meant that the person belonging to the voice was searching. "I don't see anything," he finally announced in the same soft-spoken manner so as not to alarm me. "Check again." The first quiver in my voice was a sign of nervousness. "It's near Cook." "I'm sorry, my map does not show it. Oh, I see," he finally exclaimed. "Yes, there is no AAA service in Cook, but I *am* showing Warroad, yes, that's the next town, Warroad." "Where's Warroad?" I asked Tom over my shoulder. My nervousness had been contagious. Tom had drawn closer and was listening to the conversation. He signaled wildly: "No, no, we don't want Warroad, that's five hours west!" "Well, we have Duluth," the voice tried again. That was 130 miles south. The confidence I had so blindly placed in the system was shaken. The man at the other end continued the electronic search for better alternatives. While doing so, he made polite conversation: "How's the weather up there?" "Thirty-three below," was my curt and proud reply. "Oh, my, how can you *stand* it? Here in Florida it's seventy degrees."

I had reached a central station in Florida that handled emergency calls from all over the country. Gone was my illusion of a friendly helper who would come from a neighboring town to bail us out. "Never mind!" I felt the familiar sensation in the back of my head, indicating that a tension headache was creeping up my neck and taking hold of me. "Never mind. We'll figure it out." "We'll be happy to help and to serve you," the well-trained voice continued. I slammed the receiver down and sank helplessly into the green wicker chair. What now? We were stuck and it was thirty below. We would never get out of here.

"Wait," Tom's face lit up. "I know. Let's call Mike. He has a rusty pickup with a snowplow and a tow cable. Maybe he can help." We checked our watches and decided that since it was ten in the morning, it was an appropriate time to call. Of course he would assist us, was Mike's immediate answer. Just come on over. But don't hurry, because we'll get to it when it warms up, a little after eleven. "Warming up," in the local lingo, meant that the thermometer would painfully inch up three or four degrees around noon before plunging again. Yet, comforted by Mike's words, we concluded that the neighbor was ready and willing to help while all those electronically run, corporate systems never worked out.

We trudged down the snow-covered road and met Mike at his front door. "Nice to see you," he muttered. "How've you been. Come in for a cup of coffee. Well, let's see," he added, scratching his head and consulting his watch, "it's a quarter to eleven. We've got plenty of time to spare. I guess it's time for a beer." This was a ritual, and we knew we could not avoid it. So we sat on Mike's barstools in the kitchen and toasted the success of the operation to come. Lonnie, "the wife," was over taking care of the Lowell sisters, the elderly women who lived a couple of miles down the river, he informed us. Winter was getting a bit tough for them. The grass-roots community network seemed to surpass anything that would come from a telephone call to 1-800-AAA-HELP.

One beer was followed by another, and we were pretty tipsy when we finally began our rescue operation. Mike started up the rusty pickup, whose bed was loaded with cement blocks for added traction, and backed it out of his immaculate garage (the latter, together with short-cropped grass, was a status symbol in the North Woods). At the bottom of the hill, he revved the engine and, with the grip provided by the extra weight and a pair of snow chains, in one go made it up the hill to the stranded car. With a minimum of effort, he hooked it up to his truck, and within five minutes, while we watched in awe, our trapped vehicle was back on track, gently rolling downhill behind Mike's pickup. It looked like a docile duckie behind the mama duck. Well, congratulations! I was jubilant. Tom was dumbfounded. "I guess if I had worked on it just a little longer . . ." he began. I looked at him sideways. Would he ever accept defeat?

Cabin Opener

THE ANXIOUS AND METICULOUS ROB had left us with ample instructions on how to "open" and "close" the two cabins. In the fall we carried out the closing ceremony in reverential fashion. We had drained the oil from the Jari and the generator. The spark plugs were removed so that a few drops of penetrating oil would keep the cylinder and piston from locking in the winter freeze. We had taken off the screens and put in the storm windows. We carefully emptied the pipes of any remaining water. At the end of the day, we would crawl into bed but not without anointing our aching limbs with entire tubes of Bengay, which later was replaced by the more fashionable Flexall. Since we were going to the cabins during the winter, we gradually came to bypass those parts of the instructions that had to do with storing bedding, rearranging and covering furniture, and labeling things. At first we felt full of guilt, as if we were transgressing some maternal law concerning linens and cushions, but we came to appreciate the shortcuts.

If closings were difficult and tedious, openings were more cheerful. The long winter was coming to an end, spring was rushing in, and everywhere nature began to teem with life. One bright afternoon in early May, we arrived for what we had dubbed the "Cabin Opener," fully intent on carrying out our many tasks. Among the sometimes subtle pleasures these various rites afforded was the reassurance of cycles. Openers were a sign of stability in life, of an order one could count on. In addition, they promised adventures to come.

Although we spent quite a bit of time at our cabin in the winter, that first arrival in spring was always special. This year again, we were elated by the scene as we looked upriver. The snow had completely melted since our last visit, the grass was pushing up, and aspen shoots were growing all over the portion we called our "lawn." The old willow trees had fresh yellow branches and tender buttons. The tips of the spruce branches were heavy with buds, and the aspen leaves were ready to unfold. Birds were singing and twittering everywhere. The river was dark and swift. It looked as if the ice had broken not long before. Occasional traces of ice pushed toward shore. It would be a chilly swim, I remarked. As we approached the cabin, black-capped chickadees buzzed us. Their joyful song, *chick-a-dee-dee,* seemed to say, "Where is my food, where is my food?" Tom's first move was toward the barrel that contained sunflower seeds. He appeased the little birds by filling the feeder. The tone of their songs changed. Now they were saying, "*Fee-bee, fee-bee,* food, glorious food."

No sooner had Tom fulfilled this obligation than a hummingbird, its shiny red throat and green back glistening in the morning light, flew toward the cabin and stopped right in front of him. It turned its head to look at Tom: "Where is my feeder, *twit, twit?*" it seemed to ask, while it hovered in midair with its wings humming. The tiny bird with its needlelike bill and delicate feet was beating its wings seventy-five times per second, according to the bird book. It flew backward a few inches, as if to give Tom space to go and ready the tubular plastic hummingbird feeder. He filled it with a dark red liquid that he had concocted by adding water to a red powder with plenty of sugar. He hung it outside, right next to the window under the eave, and very soon, the first client arrived. Just back from Guatemala or perhaps from even farther away, the hummer made the rounds of the feeder's plastic petals with their fake yellow pistils into which it inserted its bill. It even paused a few times, its feet delicately resting on the bars below the pistils, and peered inside the cabin as if to check us out. We held our breath until our first visitor departed. Soon there was a steady rhythm of comings and goings. Monsieur and Madame, as we had baptized the couple, were replenishing themselves after their long journey. They were setting up house, a tiny little nest in which Madame, with her burnished gray breast, and without Monsieur's ruby throat, but a creature no less delicate than her mate, had laid a couple of pea-sized eggs out of which more hummers would come to join their parents at the feeder near the window.

Meanwhile, we registered a steady stream of birds to and from the feeder. The birds first landed in the tall aspen trees near the river and reconnoitered. Was it safe? Then, they approached one by one and perched in the old balsams nearby. Soon after, if they traveled in a group, as most did, they sent a scout. If that one approved of the food and thought it was safe, the rest of the birds followed. This was a busy time of year. Driven by hunger, the birds that had stayed in the area during winter, like the chickadees and the jays, came out of the woods, where not much was growing yet, in search of food near human habitat and in open areas. They were joined by the birds that returned for the summer from their southern camps, blackbirds and pine siskins, as well as by those that, like the chunky, friendly evening grosbeaks, were passing through on their way even farther north into Canada and who needed to replenish themselves. Those birds usually lingered and let the weather warm up before they flew north.

Traffic at the feeder was dense. A flock of grosbeaks had just arrived. The males were brighter yellow and sported white patches on their wings; the females were a drabber olive. Their shrill whistle first sounded high up in the aspens before they converged upon the feeder. They squatted in the bird house and filled their large, conical bills with gobs of striped sunflower seeds. Their visible contentment was contagious. At times, they accepted a chickadee, a nuthatch, or a dark-streaked pine siskin on the platform with them. Mostly, they chased other birds away and refused to leave until they were done eating.

The red-winged blackbirds, their bright chevrons at the forefront of their wings, were the most aggressive. When their call, transcribed in bird books as *o-ka-lee,* resonated, all the other birds listened and prepared to leave. We had seen blackbirds chase ravens and even eagles out of their nesting area. They did not respect hierarchy based on size and were feisty at the feeder. Not even the blue jays, usually the despots of the feeder, were able to upstage the blackbirds. The blackbirds took over and let no other birds in. In addition, they fought viciously among themselves for a prime spot on the platform. The scene was far from peaceful. From our porch we could almost see and hear the birds' bills crushing the seeds. After a flock left and before the arrival of the next, only the unperturbed chickadees kept cheerfully coming and going, from the low-hanging branches of the spruce tree to the feeder and back.

Each year, different groups dominated. This year, blue jays came in large numbers, announcing their visits with one of their multiple, raucous action songs. They sat in the feeder like musketeers or swashbucklers, shaking their tufted heads and large bills from side to side, squandering a lot of seeds in the process. Some local people did not like the jays because they were in the habit of filling their cheek pouches with seeds and carry them off into the woods. Later, they would not remember where the seeds were. It was, one could argue in their favor, their way of planting trees. Although less aggressive than the blackbirds, the jays also commanded the field, and when they arrived, the smaller birds promptly got out of their way.

When, the following day, Tom stepped out onto the porch to set the table for breakfast, he froze and gestured me to hush and join him. I tiptoed out. Tom pointed to the old aspen with bare branches that stood less than twenty feet from the cabin. There a bald eagle was sitting, surveying the activity along the river. Seen so close, his size became imposing. Indeed, while he was sitting on the branch right in front of us, we could almost feel his talons on our skin. The eagle's white head rotated at a 180-degree angle, back and forth, back and forth. We stood motionless under the bird's spell. He finally saw or heard us and flew off, revealing the full extent of his wingspan. We were free to breathe again. What a sight! The tall dead tree was one of the birds' favorite trees. We learned how all the dead trees were important for habitat. That aspen seemed to be everyone's favorite, from the cocky kingfisher to the phoebe and now the eagle, all of which sat on its upper branches. Even the finches and the chickadees, not to mention the jays, elected its barren rungs, the bark of which had been worn off by the sheer number of bird claws of all sizes landing on it.

Tom was out and about, pouring oil into the crankcases, filling tanks with gas, reconnecting wires, and cleaning spark plugs. I went to help him install the screens. After several hours, exhausted and exhilarated, we finally took out Rob and Louise's vintage lawn chairs and sank into them, overlooking the newly open river moving swiftly at the bottom of the hill. We were intrigued by a rapidly repeated, slightly nasal sound. It stopped and started, stopped and started. Then a beaver climbed onto a fallen log in the water. It ambled along the trunk, foraging around. Soon another, larger specimen came swimming from the direction of the beaver house. Only its head—that is, its eyes and ears—was visible. The larger beaver making the funny sounds now climbed onto the same log with his companion and began nuzzling her. It was a couple courting in the first spring breeze.

"How cute," I exclaimed. I was so moved by the beavers' display of affection that I completely forgot my official feeling of ambivalence toward them, acquired during an earlier skiing expedition. We watched the pair as they crawled up and down the log, swam around, and made what in our interpretation were happy noises at each other. They seemed really content to have found each other in this wide open space without needing to burrow through tunnels and hack their way out through thick ice. Clearly, they had spring fever.

And their spring fever was contagious. The whole world seemed to be bursting with life. The wind was blowing gently from the south, bringing in warmer air. The trees groaned, sap rising up their long trunks and into their branches eighty feet above. Insects were humming, and bird cries filled the air. Soon the peepers came out and chirped throughout the night. To his uninformed spouse, Tom had earlier explained that those were little frogs that were going to peep all night long. There were thousands of them. It was true, nature did everything in abundance. Only a few would survive, however; most would provide food for fish, birds, and turtles in a greater chain of being.

With all the excitement in nature, we felt our own chests swell with emotion as we sat out in the first warm evening breeze. We lingered and watched the sun set, already farther west, closer to the intersection of the two riverbanks, where it would vanish at the solstice in barely another couple of months.

Tree-Planting Ceremony

Tree planting was to become another major ritual. Rob had left us a thick report on forest management drawn up by the state Department of Natural Resources. As a purist (or "eco-freak," in the local idiom), Rob had wanted to "restore the wilderness" by introducing more diversity. An agent of the DNR had prepared a complete "inventory" of the property, with illustrations, maps, and recommendations, one of which was that the Morrows create more habitat for different kinds of wildlife by planting bushes and diversifying the species of trees. Because of two successive clear cuttings, aspens were beginning to outnumber all other species. This, in turn, had repercussions on the wildlife. Beavers especially, the report confirmed, were thriving: several generations had indeed successfully "logged" the aspens along the river in front of the cabin. Since their industry had improved our view and it all seemed to have happened a long time ago, we did not give it that much thought—yet. The DNR manual, however, recommended planting red pine trees as well as some bushes—high cranberry and bunchberries—that did not appeal to the beavers in order to discourage them from expanding, not only along the river, but also up the creeks.

Rob had begun this work along the river, and we took it upon ourselves to carry on by dutifully planting various kinds of trees every spring. It was our way of paying tribute to Rob and to the environment, as well as improving the property. Feeling virtuous on every point, we made the activity into a yearly happening that quickly became known as "the tree-planting ceremony." It took place in early May, but actually began the fall before.

Trees had to be ordered from a mailing list sent out by one of several state nurseries under the direction of the DNR. One could order either seedlings or transplants, the difference between them being one of size and price. For any order, the minimum purchase was a mere five hundred trees. In addition to the size of the plants, the order size also depended on the species. Red and white pines came in larger numbers, as did white and black spruces. Some of the rarer species, such as tamarack, could be ordered in smaller quantities. Tom took special pleasure in meticulously filling out the forms. Prone to quantitative thinking, he found choosing and counting blissful occupations. The suspense increased when, in mid-April, the card arrived in the mail that gave the date and location of the pickup. For best results, the trees had to be planted within seventy-two hours of leaving the nursery.

The day following the pickup of our precious cargo, we rose at the crack of dawn to do our planting. For the occasion Tom had ordered, from one of the numerous specialty catalogs left by Rob, a bright yellow hard hat and a spade used to make a gash in the cold ground into which the baby trees could be inserted. The sun was just casting its first rays when, after a solid breakfast of eggs and hash browns—after all, we were going to be doing heavy-duty work and would not be bothered by cholesterol—we set out. The warmer weather had already brought out the blackflies. They were vicious at this time of the year, biting every area of exposed skin and injecting a chemical that kept blood from coagulating. In addition to the protective jeans, long-sleeved shirts, hats, and bandanas we put on, I wore my mosquito helmet with a net that covered my face and neck and made me look like a medieval knight. Tom was brave, and in keeping with his manly image, refused such cowardly devices.

First, we removed the seedlings from their plastic-lined boxes, put them all in buckets with water, and hurried out to the field. There, the main part of the ceremony could begin. While one of us—usually Tom—made a gash in the ground, the other took a seedling or transplant and set it in the small opening, taking care not to crimp the roots, which had to extend into the cold clay soil beneath the cover of leaves and detritus. Then the spade was inserted again, this time behind the seedling, and twisted sideways to close the hole. At least in theory, a little water was needed to ensure that the roots would be moist.

After more than a half day's work, and with our limbs aching, we had emptied only two boxes, which meant we had eight hundred seedlings and transplants to go. Wistfully, we were stumbling back to the cabin for lunch when our friend Tim appeared with a friend in tow. He was waving from afar, giving us one of his big smiles under his flaxen curls: "Hi, guys! We're here to help." I glanced at Tom, who, pleased as always to have more company, motioned that they should join us for lunch. After a hearty cabin-style sandwich that we prepared to show we were gracious hosts, Tom enthusiastically invited his guests to accompany him out to the field for the afternoon part of the planting. This would mean a well-deserved respite for me.

The threesome left in single file on the narrow trodden path out to the field. I excused myself under the pretext of some domestic chores. Making myself a midday coffee, I watched the planters move out toward the field. Tom was leading the troupe, waving his arms, pointing to bushes and shrubs, and showing off his newly acquired skills in arboreal nomenclature. Tim was walking close behind, seemingly absorbing the master's words with great eagerness. Paul, who brought up the rear, looked like a little kid lagging behind. It was clear that his idea of fun in the wilderness had little if anything to do with planting trees.

Seated in one of the Windsor chairs on the porch I chuckled, stirring the cream in my coffee, and watching the men through my binoculars. At first, they kept to a clear division of labor. Paul took the seedlings from the bucket and handed them, one by one, to Tim. The latter put them delicately into the spots prepared by Tom, who, following his temperament and the rules of hospitality, had reserved the big job for himself. Soon I observed how Paul began looking around, twiddling the tiny seedlings in his hands, obviously quite bored. I could not hear the sound track because of the distance, but from what I could see, I could imagine Paul's hmms and ohs! to what Tom was saying. Tim still feigned interest. Tom must have been giving one of his speeches about nature and seemed unperturbed by what I could detect as the gradual disaffection of his crew. With unflagging enthusiasm and without giving in to the flies, whose presence I guessed from the repeated hand motions, Tom surged ahead, plunging his spade into the barely unfrozen ground and indulging in his favorite activity— first counting the trees they had planted and then multiplying the number (by two) of the gashes and sutures in the earth.

While still dividing my attention between my coffee and the scene in the distance, I heard some loud thumping and rustling noises coming from behind the cabin. Deer? A bear? I saw a dark shape, I held my breath, then a man appeared. Should I grab the rifle again, just like on the day of the bear? The man was slightly stooped and wore a crumpled little hat, from which protruded a mass of black curly hair streaked with white. Dark-rimmed glasses adorned his face, and he was wearing sports clothes with a checkered flannel shirt. He waved his arms—"Hello there!" It was another friend, Allan, the movie buff. Buoyed by relief, I limply managed to wave back.

Allan had been a journalist with a major newspaper, but he did not get along with the bosses and was now freelancing, writing about films, a subject he adored and one that led him all over the world. It must have been on just one of these trips that he had met Ingrid, the woman whose outline was just now emerging from among the trees. Ingrid was from Germany, and though she was from the south, she had many of the characteristics associated with the northern part of that nation: energy, endurance, resistance to cold (as I could observe a little later when she went for a lengthy swim in the frigid river). Introductions were quickly made, and the newcomers announced that they too, upon Tom's invitation, had come to help with the planting. With so many hands, surely all of the tiny trees would make it into the ground in short order.

Allan and Ingrid headed out to the field and soon could be seen talking with the others. After much palaver—but little action—the group broke up, and Tim and Paul as well as Allan and Ingrid returned to the cabin and broke the news to me that I myself was wanted in the field by Tom. At the same time, Tim and Paul announced their decision to call it quits for the day so that they could go canoeing on this "imposing river." Ingrid unveiled her plan to swim despite my warning about ice-cold waters and strong currents. Reluctantly, I put my mosquito helmet back on and shuffled out to the field. Tom muttered something about the absence of reliable helpers. Then the two of us, braving the heat, the sun, and the blackflies that somehow had made it under our sweatshirts and even into my helmet, began in rather biblical fashion our rhythmic task of making a gash, pulling a seedling out of a pail, putting it into the cold ground, and closing the gash.

After a while, we almost got used to the flies. In this new phase of coexistence, I even found time to look around, enjoy the brilliant sunlight, the deep blue skies, and the river, on which the wind was chasing dark swirls of water. I heard the honking of geese on their annual migration to Canada. Those are real geese, unlike the ones that flew from pond to pond in front of corporate offices along the city bypasses into suburban sprawl, Tom declared solemnly. The always curious chickadees came by to inspect our work. The sun began to set over the tall trees on the other side of the river. In the distance I saw Ingrid splashing in the water while Allan supervised from the red rock. Tim and Paul were gliding downstream in our canoe as we were toiling away, bloody sweat running down our bitten faces. Turning from these illusions of harmony I focused on my tree-planting duties while wiping my forehead. Seven hundred fifty down, but just as many to go.

Later, much later, we dragged our aching bodies back to the cabin. It came as no surprise that it was up to us to do all the "homestyle cooking," for ourselves as well as for our self-proclaimed helpers. After all, we were the hosts.

We too were the ones who rose early the next day to serve everyone pancakes before we headed out to the field alone, having waved off fake offers of "Oh, but we'll help you!" The second day was even hotter. The flies were worse than ever, but now we were on a countdown. We spurred each other on to see how many of the five hundred remaining seedlings we could plant in record time. When night fell, we were down to two hundred and fifty. Our friends had long left and were on their way back to the city. After a rather silent dinner, we stumbled into our bed. All night long, I had sweet dreams of repetitive motion syndrome: open, insert, close, open, insert, close, open, insert, close . . .

Bruno the Bear

HE FIRST APPEARED DURING TREE PLANTING. we were just lingering on the porch with our would-be helpers—Allan, Ingrid, Tim, and Paul—after a pancake breakfast that would restore energy to our tired bodies for another demanding day. The cub came out of nowhere, arriving so silently that none of us heard him approach. The little bear was just suddenly there, at the wooden bird feeder that stands on a pole thirty feet from the cabin. He was the size of a dog, a labrador, perhaps. He had to rear up on his hind legs to reach the feeder, on which Tom, every morning, put out a new batch of sunflower seeds, ostentibly for the birds. Since no mother bear appeared, we concluded that he was an orphan and our hearts went out to him. The bear was scooping up the seeds with his front paws. When this method did not go fast enough, he stuck out his long purple tongue, which enabled him to lap up gobs of seeds at a time.

We watched every move of the "cute little thing," as Allan put it, that was plundering the feeder. We all tiptoed taking pictures. The bear never even glanced in our direction. After emptying the feeder, he flopped facedown on the grass and, with his front paws and tongue, gobbled up the seeds that had fallen to the ground. He finally ambled away, shaking his haunches, and disappeared behind the hawthorn bushes.

Tim, an animal rights advocate who specialized in carrying mosquitoes from the cabin to the great outdoors in order not to squash them (which prompted us to take sadistic delight in slapping them right in front of him), gushed with sentimental praise of the bear. What a cute little thing, he kept saying, seconded by Paul and Ingrid. Allan, with his usual good humor, baptized the cub Bruno, and for the next couple of years, Bruno was our neighbor, a pet, a pest, and, when guests were present, our best tourist attraction.

Bruno returned a few more times that day. He looked like the friendly family dog and soon was treated as such. At dinnertime, while we were roasting some pieces of chicken over the open fire, he happened by and looked longingly in the direction of the smell and the smoke. He saw the cooks sitting around and decided to keep his distance. But from then on, he included the bird feeder in his rounds so that it had to be replenished at least a couple of times a day. I wanted to bring the seeds inside, but was overruled by the chorus, who felt the bear was a "growing fella" who needed his food. It was only fair that we contributed a little to his well-being.

And so it went. Bruno rapidly became a fixture of the cabin scene who clearly considered himself part of the household. We began to talk to him and reason with him when he misbehaved, that is, when his greed pushed him to leave nothing for the poor birds. He amused our guests seemingly on command, climbing trees, tumbling on the grass, bowling with geranium pots, and moodily shuffling up the path behind the cabin, shaking his rear end as if he were wearing oversized pants that broke over his claws. He would suddenly appear when we were walking out to the swimming point. He especially had a knack for coming out of nowhere as if to greet us when we were on our way to the outhouse. Another time I was gathering wildflowers in the field behind a gentle slope when I heard a thumping sound and looked up to see two ears and then a face appear over the hill. Bruno came straight at me, overjoyed to see me. I dropped my elaborate bouquet and bolted for the cabin, tripping over logs and stumbling into the creek. I had long lost my initial fear of bears, but our unexpected encounter in the open had nonetheless startled me.

At first, Bruno did look like a storybook teddy bear. His ears were rounded, like those of stuffed teddies. His snout was a bit longer and light brown. His deep eyes looked at us in an inquisitive, at times seemingly puzzled fashion. His shiny black fur, tiny tail, and big paws did everything to endear him to us. He must have incorporated other human outposts on his rounds, because he seemed particularly friendly and well disposed toward people. I, who always lived in the future, speculated fearfully that Bruno's absence of fear could bring him disaster at hunting season. I strongly suspected Dorothy Maloney, an elderly woman who lived alone, a kind of hippie born too early and reaching middle age too late, whose small cabin was on the county road about two miles from our place as the crow flies. Dorothy, a modern-day Saint Francis, fed feral cats, a stray dog, birds, and now, apparently Bruno, to make her existence a little less solitary. I was sure she fed him.

Bruno, in the meantime did not seem to have a single care. This was a good summer with plenty of berries, ants, mice, and whatever else could be found to round out his diet and fill his belly, especially the sunflower seeds for which he had developed a special liking. He came by every two days. Bears, Tom explained to me after consulting the Audubon book on North American mammals, need large territories, at least one square mile per bear. They patrol their territory and, within its limits, are totally serendipitous in what they eat. Their passage can be detected from ransacked anthills as well as gigantic heaps of scat.

As Bruno grew, his treatment of the feeder began to require constant repairs. We knew when he had been by even before looking closely. The feeder would be tilting, the roof turned sideways. Later, as Bruno's paws doubled in size, he tore the roof off a few times. On each occasion, Tom patiently nailed it back on. Our routine now included bringing the feeder in at night, so as to prevent damage from Bruno's rampages.

When he came by during the day, and we were around, we rushed to unscrew the feeder while alarmed birds were scattering and squirrels were scurrying. The feeder was in the porch more than it was outside, and the birds were protesting their treatment. When Bruno saw that he had been thwarted, he sat down for a few minutes while casting accusing glances in our direction. Then in the midst of my scolding—"Bad bear, bad, bad bear"—he slowly turned and walked toward the woods, always in the direction of the clothesline strung between two dead birch trees from which multicolored bathing suits and towels were hanging. One by one Bruno would tear them down, all the while looking defiantly in our direction. Then he would turn his big rump toward us and disappear between the bushes, though never for long.

We met Bruno at the swimming hole, shaking the water off his shimmering fur, or out berry picking, and later, when we were gathering bushels of bright yellow chanterelles. He was totally unafraid of humans and was constantly being photographed. One could tell that he liked to perform. For our visitors he climbed up the old balsam tree right next to the cabin, or sat on his hind legs and then sped off with his back feet touching down well ahead of his front paws.

Bruno woke us at night when he was rummaging around outside the cabin. I would go out with a flashlight and bang pots and pans to scare him off and prevent him from damaging things with his claws. The items ranged from plastic water jugs to toolboxes, beer bottles, which he shook out of their cardboard boxes, and, especially, window screens. They were his favorite. With the extra holes punched by Bruno, each night more and more mosquitoes got in. We could no longer keep up with repairs. It seemed as if we were spending most of our time undoing what Bruno did when no one was around or when we were sleeping. Nonetheless, he was cute, and in the end it was impossible to be tough with him.

One night when we were having dinner on the porch, we heard

rustling and kept silent to see where it was coming from. Our dinner table on the porch was right near the open sliding window, separated from the outside by only a thin screen. Suddenly, what popped up in front of the screen but Bruno's head! I could not remember afterward what came first, the paws or the round ears. Whatever, there he was, standing up against the window, holding on to the sill, and pressing his snout against the screen to check out the scene. He was breathing heavily, his exhalations redolent of fresh forest mixed with rotten food. I was by now accustomed to him and was far from the panic I experienced on my first day, when I ran for the shotgun after spotting my first bear. We both sat motionless while Bruno kept on looking and looking. Eventually he got tired of his position, and since nothing was forthcoming, he disappeared into the night.

Our attachment to Bruno outweighed these inconveniences. We were dreading the upcoming bear season, which lasted through the first two weeks of September. The previous year, more than four hundred bears had been registered by hunters in our area. I even wanted to take down some of the bait stations that hunters had built along possible bear paths. Bear hunting was the lowest sport, I expounded. It was hardly even a sport. You put garbage— especially old grease from restaurants, along with smelly refuse of any kind—out in the open in the same spot for a number of weeks. It would attract bears, and one day, after the season opened, you would just go there, wait for an unsuspecting victim, and shoot it. The level of chance was almost nil. And we knew that Bruno went wherever there was food.

Bruno survived the hunt, however, at least for his first year and for several more to come.

Blueberry Hill

S UMMER WAS GETTING ON, and there was much excitement in
the air about the upcoming blueberry and raspberry harvests.
We rejoiced that life in the North Woods was still governed by natural cycles and preserved some of its age-old stability. Every season
was different, the old-timers assured us, but there was also the
pleasure of habit, of starting to perceive differences and variations
in the yearly repetitions. Rituals and ceremonies kept the social
fabric intact and made this a good place to live, the locals proudly
informed us, far from the speed and decadence of city life.

We set out one afternoon in late July, ready to make the trip to
Blueberry Hill. Tom was carrying his ax and joked about how it
was symbolic in cultural theory of the opening to new ideas. He
chuckled at his own wit as he cut small branches from the trees
in order to facilitate our passage. We stopped here and there to
inspect mushrooms that grew in abundance on grassy knolls and
fallen logs.

We tramped through swampy areas, venting our displeasure as
the water slowly but inexorably seeped in through our boots; balanced on planks that spanned narrow creeks; wound our way by

some tall spruces that, we would learn later, were over a hundred and fifty years old; past the fork that led to our skiing area, out of our forest, and up a steep, narrow path overhung with spruce branches that gave Tom another opportunity to swing his ax. Unrelenting, we were making our way up to the blueberries that grew on a rocky hill where hundred-foot-tall red and white pines stood. The brush was thick and the tall grass hid downed trees over which we stumbled, landing on all fours. Nothing could deter Tom from his goal, not even bloody knees and scratches on his hands and forehead. My protests went for naught. In spite of my lifelong passion for the forest, my vision did not include thorny branches, rocks, holes, and swarms of mosquitoes and flies, not to mention the threat of predatory animals.

The vital thing was to find the little path that bordered the beaver pond and along which we had discovered the moss-covered remains of a trapper's cabin. We had missed it one day recently and, after much meandering, had ended up on a road several miles east. That had been good luck, actually. We could have traveled for several days into the Boundary Waters without ever finding a way out. I excitedly thought of my childhood characters who sent up smoke signals. We could have tested our survival skills by eating roots, leaves, grasshoppers, even mosquitoes. I could see us, as if in a movie, waving to a helicopter that had come searching for us but that just kept overlooking us. Since that day, Tom was careful to pack the compass with the picnic and I brought along bright pink ribbons.

I was reminiscing about this incident, tying ribbons on low branches while Tom, unperturbed, was surging ahead, blazing the trail with his ax. Suddenly there was a thumping noise in the woods to our left. A dark flash, a rounded head, and two black ears standing erect were briefly outlined, then the form turned and dashed off into the thicket. A little bear! My instinct was to go in his direction. Tom, at this moment the wiser of the two of us, held me back. Where there's a cub, there must be a mother, he warned.

No sooner had he said this than we saw a massive dark shape

fifteen feet away, getting taller and stretching to the sky. It was Mama Bear—and she was standing up. She must have weighed over four hundred pounds, and was in no joking mood. She growled in our direction and we froze. Tom was clutching the ax; I dropped our orange cooler on the moss-covered ground, which, thank heavens, absorbed the noise. Mama Bear tossed her head, looking at us out of her sunken, reddish eyes, undecided about what move to make next. We heard her rumble. Tom motioned to me to slowly, without losing sight of where Mama was, walk out of her area. This tactic proved successful. For several more minutes, after we could no longer see her, we heard more thumping noises, but they faded off in the opposite direction.

We continued in silence for several minutes before we paused and, finally, began to speak. I sank to the ground, exhausted. My heart was pounding so hard that I felt it was going to explode. All my recent expertise with bears had evaporated. Never run, Tom, always strong on theory, reminded me; it will only invite the bear to come after you, and in spite of their size, bears can go at more than fifteen miles an hour, at least for a while. They will most certainly outrun you. It would not have been much of a choice. Little by little, as we walked alongside the beaver pond, of which we caught glances through the thick branches, we began to breathe normally again, and soon we were laughing about Mama's tall and stylish figure. But all afternoon, whenever there was a rustling of leaves or a cracking of branches, we thought we glimpsed the tall, dark outline of Mama's imposing shape.

The berry patch Tom had in mind was beyond the trapper's cabin. I liked to rummage through a pile of half-buried bottles and cans, the remnants of his years spent far from other humans. The trapper's place furnished the first of a lot of evidence of hard drinking in earlier decades in the woods. Whiskey and aspirin, we continued to joke upon finding new evidence protruding from the ground, must have been the staff of life. Our cabin was rapidly becoming a museum of antique liquor bottles—Old Quaker, Old Log Cabin, Old Raven—read some of the names pressed into the glass flasks retrieved from the trapper's cabin as well as from earlier logging sites in nearby forest areas.

Finally, we reached the point where we had to leave the path and ascend sharply to Blueberry Hill, where Tom hoped to find this year's cache. We started our climb through thick brush and over loose boulders, across large, smooth, rocky surfaces, and all the way to the top, up a gradient of about four hundred feet over a quarter mile where some first-growth white pines stood. We reached the open part from which the forest stretched out in front of us, seemingly endlessly. Not one human construction was in sight. Only countless wooded ridges, sharply demarcated by the angle of the sunlight, stood out with their various shadings of dark and light green, and nearer us, a stretch of river, glistening in the sun. The only sound was that of the wind that made the pines truly "whisper," a sound quite different from the rustling of the aspen leaves at the bottom of the hill. We stood there for a few minutes, taking in the scene and letting our thoughts roam freely.

Then we both became practical. We had built up hefty appetites from our trek across the forest and our encounter with Mama Bear. We looked around for a log that would serve as a picnic bench. We found the remains of a fallen pine on which we could sit and overlook the hills, the beaver pond, and the river in the distance. Tom uncorked a bottle of red wine; we passed it between us and felt the warmth of the liquid in our veins. Homemade bread and Italian salami completed the feast. It caused us to fondly remember the winter day on which a whiskey jack—a Canadian jay—came to beg for some food, took a slice of salami we had thrown onto the snow, and flew off with it to a distant branch, where he shared it with his companion. Today no whiskey jacks were present for the tasting. Only the chickadees came and signaled to us in their friendly twitter that they too were interested in joining our feast. After our luncheon we felt ready to harvest the berries that seemed to be growing everywhere.

Tom's hunch proved right. On top of the hill, among the boulders as well as on the steep sides, blueberry plants abounded and the season was good. We went to work. Each of us started on a patch, and then we continued on to several more of them, sliding our fingers through the branches, separating the berries from the stems, and dropping them into our small buckets. The contents of these buckets were then transferred to the orange cooler that, because of its bright color, served as a rallying point for our huntings and gatherings. Several times we heard rustling and thumping nearby and thought of Mama Bear, but she never showed. We found huge piles of bear droppings filled with half-digested blueberries; many anthills had been broken into as well.

The sun was already quite low when I decided that I had put in a day's work. I sat down and watched the sun. The colors became darker and the shadows longer. The wind picked up for a while. The birds were fluttering around, feeding before bedtime. Once again, I had the fleeting sensation less of harmony, perhaps, than of being part of a vast expanse of nature. There weren't even any mosquitoes to disturb this feeling.

It was dark when, tired and hungry, but happy after our day's labor, we straggled back to the cabin with our loot. The cooler was filled to the brim with precious berries. Several more outings were organized, each of them just as literally fruitful. When, after a week, the picking became slim, we turned to jam making. Tom, who was prone to counting, was boasting to everyone: forty-eight jars! Throughout the winter while sitting in our city kitchen, watching the snow drift by outside, we would be able to see and taste the great outdoors and our beloved Blueberry Hill.

Raspberry Picking

Wɪᴛʜ ᴀ ɴᴇᴡ sᴇɴsᴇ ᴏꜰ ᴛɪᴍᴇ, we watched with great eagerness the ripening of the raspberries at the end of our field.
It looked like a banner year. By early August, we decided that the
moment had come. We struggled across the field, through the
knee-high grass, not without pausing to admire the seedlings we
had planted literally by the sweat of our brows. Had they grown
a quarter of an inch? Were they too dry? There had been some
rain since they were planted. Water was crucial immediately after
planting, Tom declared, full of his new knowledge. He thought the
seedlings looked a good two inches taller. I was, as always, more
skeptical. But the seedlings had grown—that was a fact—and the
survival rate was good. We noted this with satisfaction, before we
knew that trees always do well until winter, until February, to be
exact, when they fall prey less to the cold than to hungry deer who
have exhausted all other sources of nourishment. The seedlings
are stunted and need an entire season just to grow back, only to be
devoured again the following winter. Deer seemed especially fond
of young jack pines. They chewed them down to their bare stems,
but each year the trees came back. After several such croppings,

they began to look more like bushes. Tom liked to joke about our round, squat "jack bushes." The deer gave jack pines a "gnarled" look that appealed to human emotions and inspired stories and poems of nature. Only now did we find out that this look was more cultivated than natural.

Finally, we arrived at the raspberry field. Raspberries, I learned, like areas opened by the recent clearing of forest. They often grow where trees have been decimated, either by loggers or, in this case, by beavers. These patches would last, perhaps for a decade, until new trees and taller bushes, mountain maple, chokecherries, and even alder or willow, filled in the area. At least the beavers are good for something, Tom laughed, as he put down the old orange cooler that would receive the booty. He opened the snap top and took out two aluminum bowls, one of which he handed to me. We went in in different directions and started picking.

It was a silent operation. Brushing aside the tall grasses, I discovered an entire world down below. The bushes and tall grasses were like the top canopy of a rain forest. Underneath, there were progressive layers of subcanopies, all the way down to the moss cover of the moist ground. At the level of the berries, there unfolded in front of me an unknown but vital configuration of vegetation, beetles, ants, worms of all sizes, shapes, and colors. Each time I gently lifted a branch to remove its precious cargo, scores of beetles scurried away or dropped to the ground, into what seemed like a bottomless pit.

I let the berries fall straight into the bowl. Tiny worms, green or white, lifted their heads and tried to crawl toward the light and freedom. I looked at my bowl and its various occupants with mixed reactions. In nature, nothing came in as pure and aseptic a way as in the store or even in pictures. Wild rice, I remembered, had been full of spiders and worms, a whole ecosystem that had been vanquished from my urban environment by deadly "cleaning" products. Knowledgeable as ever, Tom informed me that the greater percentage of the globe was covered by insects, rodents, worms, and fungi. They were probably more precious in the food chain than humans. Without them, birds and mammals could not exist. A healthy environment could be measured by a higher density of insects and rodents.

While picking the berries, I disturbed spiders that had staked out a good niche for their webs in the forks of delicate branches. It seemed that I was ruthlessly disturbing all these carefully constructed habitats that the creatures had to rebuild all over again after my greedy passage. This destructive part of berry picking did not appeal to me. Or perhaps I was using that as an excuse because I was lazy and felt that we would be better off buying our berries at the supermarket.

I looked up to find Tom, whose rounded back I discovered a few hundred yards away from me, working toward the river. Beyond him one of the eagles was spiraling downward toward the tall trees on the other side of the river. The sun was setting. About a month ago it had reached what seemed to be the vanishing point between the two riverbanks, where the rows of spruces that lined both sides came together, and now was already starting its reverse move. The wind was blowing steadily from the north, which energized the whole countryside and prevented the mosquitoes from landing on us. By this time of the summer, the countryside was just beginning to turn yellow. I looked at the dark outline of the balsams and the orange rays of the sun. A lone star appeared. Was it Venus? I felt my soul expanding with the universe and its smells, sights, sounds, and tactile sensations.

Berry picking was not always that serene. If, by chance, the wind was not blowing but the sun was shining, or it was about to storm, picking was analogous to being martyred. From the depth of the grass would rise armies of mosquitoes that seemed to have developed natural immunity to repellent, be it in the form of spray, liquid, solid, candles, wax, or whatever. They penetrated clothes, slipped in under the mosquito nets, and, as if to defy ad campaigns about upgraded repellents, crawled mercilessly up inside our pant legs. Even worse were the deerflies that had by now replaced the blackflies and that sucked blood from one's face. Then berry picking became a battle against the elements and a struggle for survival.

After every excursion in the field, a careful inspection for ticks was the order of the day. Ticks liked to burrow in private parts, where it was nice and warm. At times we would wake up during the night and feel something crawling along our legs. If the moving "something" was approached very slowly and the hand then suddenly brought down on it, the tick could be apprehended. Ticks were so tough, if one tossed them outside the cabin, they seemed to find their way right back in. To prevent them from returning, we had to burn them or drown them in rubbing alcohol. We collected the ticks in a little shot glass that we filled with the (to them) deadly liquid. We delighted in inspecting the morgue from time to time. I also liked to tell the story of the day when I had poured a little rubbing alcohol in a shot glass, but the tick for whom it was destined had somehow managed to escape. The glass was there with its clear liquid when Tom came inside. Noticing the glass, and never one to turn down a drink, he imagined that I had poured myself a little gin and was ready to join in the tasting. He downed it and almost immediately started a frenzied dance while trying to spit up the liquid that, he claimed, was burning his insides. This had been the tick's revenge.

Devastation

THE BERRY SEASON HAD PASSED. Although the grass in the field was still green, it was taking on a more yellowish tinge. Ferns, susceptible to cold air, turned orange. Canadian thistles speckled the picture with red dots. The days were getting shorter, and the blackbirds—among the first to migrate—were gathering in flocks, a sign of their impending departure. We decided that it was time for another walk in the forest and set out with our backpack, which contained our customary lunch, a compass, an ax, plenty of mosquito repellent, and helmets.

We walked across the field along the river on the little path that animals, too, had begun to adopt, judging from all the droppings we encountered. We stopped to identify various species, always hoping for signs of wolf and moose. Sometimes our romantic longings were even rewarded. The field was covered with white and purple asters. The taller, slender goldenrods were about to open and add bright yellow splotches everywhere. Pearly everlasting, with its whitish clusters resembling little beads, was in abundance this year. In a swampier part of the field the purple petals of wild orchids emerged from the tall grasses. Not that we were particularly versed in botany; our knowledge had been recently acquired from an Audubon guide, a thoughtful present from one of our guests. We impressed each other with our newly acquired nomenclature. In addition to those of mushrooms, Tom delighted in reciting the Latin names of flowers. Since my childhood had been marred by deadly Latin classes, I could not share his enthusiasm and continued to accuse him of pedantry.

Thus "reading the book of nature," as Tom called it, we strolled down the familiar forest path, past the first creek, where the water did not seem to be moving as swiftly as in the past, a fact we promptly ascribed to the dry season. We decided to turn at the second creek and follow it all the way down to the river, over a couple of gentle hills and past tall white pines. We began to notice that this creek was not moving much either. But we were too busy climbing over logs and pushing aside branches to pay much attention to the virtual absence of flow until we reached a modest clearing, just before the two creeks come together. We emerged from the thicket and froze. Where earlier there had been a swift rivulet and tall trees, albeit with a few beaver traces, there was now a flooded area of devastation.

Hundred-foot-tall aspens had been felled and were lying helterskelter over the bed of the former creek. Some ash trees had met the same fate. From the dark, murky waters (surely a breeding ground for mosquitoes), spruces stretched their branches, covered with rusty needles, helplessly toward heaven. A giant aspen was leaning against the pine tree, making it look "messy," I complained. Many of the trees that were still standing exhibited the characteristic hourglass shape two or three feet above ground. Large shavings were scattered around the trunks. "Beavers! The beavers!" I exclaimed, adding a few expletives in front of the noun. The beavers had "wrecked" our most cherished area!

We looked over the calm waters and spotted their brand-new lodge near the western shore of the large pond, and a long, solidlooking dam in the background, just above the little waterfall. I sat down. Tom stood motionless. Our appetites were forgotten. We looked on at the destruction, insensitive to all the good reasons enumerated in authoritative nature books on why beavers are the best thing for the environment. After a while, when I came back to myself, I vowed revenge.

In silence, we trudged back to the cabin to catch our breath and deliberate on how to proceed. Tom suggested we go the official route and call the DNR. They would surely have an answer to our dilemma. We were greeted by the customary answering machine telling us that the workers were momentarily out. After many tries and several more days, our calls were finally returned by one of the local agents, who suggested a few names of possible trappers but assured us that dynamite in the winter months—though illegal—worked best. Of course we had to be careful: many an honest citizen had blown himself up or at least lost a limb in the process. If we did not like dynamite but were interested in doing the job ourselves, we would have to make "chinks" in the dam in the afternoon while the beavers were soundly sleeping in their lodge, then come back be-

fore dusk with a rifle and sit there quietly, waiting for the beavers to come and repair the dam. While they were fixing their structure, a sniper would be able to shoot them.

We were dumbfounded. What good was the DNR, if it couldn't help out taxpaying citizens, I argued. Secretly, I was anguished. I had come to the North Woods to share my existence with the fauna and flora. Now the fauna was killing my flora. I had wanted to go to nature to restore myself and leave the hassles of civilization behind. And suddenly, the beavers were "destroying" not just any forest but *our* forest. Why couldn't they have gone farther east, into the Boundary Waters proper? I remained deep in thought.

Sorting out the options, we finally decided to go for the chinks. We could not quite calm our consciences and hoped that by making a hole in their dam, we would invite the beavers to move. Tomorrow we would begin to carry out our plan. Suddenly, oneness with nature turned into division. The war on the beavers had begun!

PART II

The War against the Beavers

The War Begins

W E BECAME OBSESSED. Every day, we hiked out to the pond, falling over logs and getting scratched and whipped by limbs. Unperturbed, with blood on our foreheads and twigs in our hair, we climbed up onto the impressive dam. It was not for nothing that the beavers had earned their reputation as "nature's engineers." The mosaic of clay, branches, and rocks was proof of their ingenuity.

The beavers had chosen the spot where the creek ran through a flat area just above the waterfall. They built the dam right on top of the fall in such a way that it emerged two or three feet out of the pond on one side, but there was at least a fifteen-foot drop on the other. The dam was about forty feet long and six feet wide. A small opening at its base allowed for a little bit of flow and prevented complete stagnation. The structure was so solid that it took a huge ax and a lot of patience on our behalf just to cut a gash of more than a foot.

At first we were in awe before this wonder of nature. We remembered how books about wilderness said that American civilization was indebted to the beavers. Helen Hoover, for example, convincingly and beautifully defended their contributions to the nation's usable water and fertile soil. But those books were written decades ago, when the beavers were almost extinct. I, in turn, persuaded Tom that there were more beavers now than there had been in the eighteenth century. And just look around. Indeed, when he saw all his favorite, eighty-year-old trees getting felled so that a beaver could snatch off a little branch to put on top of their house, his indignation got the upper hand, and it was, if not happily, then at least with some determination that he hacked away at the dam.

It was hard labor. Our muscles ached and once again "the sweat of our brows" attracted swarms of blackflies that bit our faces until we bled. But little by little, we managed to open the dam so that the water flowed over the top and we could judge by the watermarks on the standing trees that the level was lower than when we arrived. We had succeeded in opening the dam. Now all we had to do was wait until evening.

And so it went time after time. Once there was a solid flow, we went back to the cabin only to return to the beaver pond after sunset. Staying there was impossible because of the mosquitoes and the flies. At dusk, the beavers would wake up, and as predicted by the DNR employee, they would come out to fix the dam. At that moment one had to sit motionless—though one was being eaten alive—and shoot as they were climbing onto the dam. A gentleman, Tom usually offered to do this run alone. Bravely and like a true woodsman, he set out with plenty of repellent and a deer rifle with a scope. Every time he arrived there, he reported, the dam had already been restored. In fact, it seemed as if it were being repaired before we even got back to our cabin.

One night, Tom thought he saw a beaver swimming and took aim at it. *Bam!* The shot reverberated in the woods. *Bam-bam-bam.* The sound grew fainter as the echo traveled among the trees. The beaver had had time to slap its tail. Tom later recounted that he saw its hind legs fly up in the air and disappear in the water. A few ripples. Then silence. Had he hit it? His adrenaline was mounting. He waited for a while, not minding being devoured alive by insects, but finally, when nothing stirred, decided to pack up and head back to the cabin.

I had been waiting faithfully, rocking on the porch. Darkness was already falling, and Tom was still nowhere in sight. It was one of those quiet nights when not even a breeze was stirring in the trees. A couple of mosquitoes were humming in the air. This was their hour, as Tom liked to declare. Then suddenly, *bam,* the sound of a shot from the vicinity of the beaver pond. I jumped. Then silence again. It was an eerie feeling. Nothing moved outside, and the darkness became even more intense. Then, suddenly a huge reddish orange ball appeared behind the trees in the distance. My heart lurched before I realized it was the moon, shedding its light over the dark, still field. It rose quickly but continued to illuminate the nightly landscape. At last, in the distance I could perceive a moving shape. I held my breath. Was it a bear? A moment of nagging doubt, then relief: no, it was Tom. I saw the shine of the rifle barrel and the bulge of a knapsack on his back. Soon he was at the door, beaming and ready to tell the tale of the beaver hunt to an eager spouse.

We never found out whether Tom had hit the beaver. There were no carcasses anywhere, and the animals' logging continued its steady course. We made many more trips to hack chinks in the dam, each time falling over logs and stepping into the deep holes on the shore that the beavers used in the winter to gain access to land from underneath the frozen water. The animals never ceased to amaze us. Each time, we chopped away, covered with mosquitoes and flies. In spite of the "damage" they did, we were ambivalent about disturbing the beavers. But the place looked more and more like a battlefield, I told myself with every inspection.

In the meantime, the beavers seemed to be expanding their territory. I complained that we had invested our savings in forested land, not in a beaver pond. So one day we spent twice the time and managed to make a sizable hole. Now the water was truly flowing and the beavers would have to move back down to the river or toward the other side, into the Boundary Waters. For that was my fantasy. The following day we were there again at our usual time. All was calm. Our jaws dropped. The dam had been repaired and the animals seemed to be sleeping happily in their house. Clearly, we were no match for the beavers.

Jim Rondeau

OUR FEELING OF ONENESS WITH NATURE was gravely compromised. After the fiasco of trying to drive the beavers out
through harassment and sabotage, we gave ourselves a few days'
respite before beginning the search for a trapper. Our neighbor
Mike, happy without a doubt that we were not "eco-freaks" like
the previous owners (little did he know about my great visions of
harmony with nature), suggested Jim Rondeau, the husband of
Lisa Rondeau, the kind woman who managed a small general store
that included the post office.

We knew Lisa well. In addition to running the store and postal
station, she was also the local analyst and the glue that held the
small community together. Many personal and collective problems were discussed and solved in her small store. With long
blond hair and sparkling gray eyes, Lisa was pretty, young, and
energetic. She took care of a family of four and countless dogs and
cats, ran the store, and found time to develop her artistic talents
by making jewelry. She sewed her own dresses and varied the local
uniform of jeans and T-shirts with ruffled, homemade skirts,
low-cut peasant blouses, and Native American–style jewelry. With

continual charm and a steady smile, Lisa was one of the pillars of our community.

Her husband Jim—Jacques—seemed to be of French Canadian origin. His ancestors must have, at some point, crossed the border, which was only a few miles away, and settled in the area. Jim had distinct French good looks with dark hair, sharp green eyes, and a broad smile. He was a survivalist of sorts, a man who chose to be without a steady job or career and to laugh at city folks who worked too hard. An avid outdoorsman whose passion was racing sled dogs—he was always going to win the next race but somehow victory eluded him—he had more than two dozen mushers in an outdoor kennel behind the house he had built for his family. The dogs, huskies of different colors, yapped whenever something or somebody stirred. The sound of their barking traveled all over and could be heard day and night. At first, before getting accustomed to the sights and sounds, we imagined rather romantically that we were hearing packs of wolves. The dogs still fooled our visitors and made them believe they were having a true wilderness experience.

Jim lived with the seasons. In the summer he was a guide. He led people into the Boundary Waters and Quetico along the border lakes and down the rivers on which the voyageurs used to canoe. He also took advantage of the berry season. Then in late August and early September, he harvested wild rice before guiding some lazy, macho tourists during bear season. And later in the year he hunted his own game—grouse and deer—to fill the family freezer for the year to come.

After we got to know him, Jim became more talkative. When we approached, he was rocking in a beat-up wicker chair on the porch of the one-story log cabin he had built to house his wife's store and the postal station, one leg slung over the armrest, and greeted us as usual: "Yeah, I don't know how you can stand it. You people are running in a rat race." With his broad grin that uncovered two rows of white, perfectly straight teeth, I found his words rather convincing. Since Tom's virility was at stake, he was more critical. Tom resorted to Aesop, declaring that Jim was a "country rat" and had to work just as much to make ends meet as we "city rats." Was he more secure than we were?

One of the newcomers, a retiree who staked his claim on the river, had been a chain saw artist. He carved regional items—owls, bears, beavers, geese, loons, welcome signs, totem poles—and sold them at Lisa's store. One morning, after a late-nighter at the Hunter's Last Chance Tavern, he took the name of the inn literally. On the way home he missed a curve, skidded on the ice, and smashed his brand-new red pickup into a tree. He was pronounced dead at the scene. When tourists returned the following season, they inquired about the sculptures. And that's how, as history quickly turned into legend, Jim became a sculptor, first of local and then of regional renown. Guiding and ricing became secondary to the artistic endeavors that began where the new neighbor's had abruptly ended. Jim even bought himself a computer and talked of setting up a Web site. He now carved everything from beavers and bears to "foreign" species, such as crocodiles and flamingos that, when displayed outside the store, looked as if they were animals who had had the good sense to anticipate global warming.

When Tom and I appealed to Jim for help in solving our beaver problem, he was still in his preartistic days. He was protective of the wilderness and was not much of a trapper. But he promised he would take a look and might be interested in beaver meat, which could serve as dog food. One evening in early September, when it was already getting dark in the late afternoon, we heard the rattle of an engine. Soon Jim emerged from the woods and was driving down the hill on an oversized four-wheeler, the back of which had been mounted with a platform to accommodate his young children, who were sitting on little benches behind bright red wooden lattices. Jim wore beige overalls, and the two youngsters had bright red woolen caps drawn down over their foreheads and ears, which gave them a tough look. With his rifle slung across the machine, Jim looked ready for action. After a brief consultation it was decided that Tom would ride with them to the trouble spot. He hopped in the back with the children. I had a good laugh after they left as I watched the machine slowly cross the field, tipping right, then left, though without spilling its human cargo before it disappeared into the thick forest.

It was already quite dark and the stars were out when Tom finally appeared on foot, alone. I immediately barraged him with questions: Where was Jim? Was he going to do it? Was he going to rid us of the beavers once and for all? Tom mumbled, but I was finally able to make out the answer. No, Jim had decreed it was too far into the woods. And why did we want to get rid of the animals anyhow? This was wilderness, after all. These critters were wilderness beavers, and it might be nice to have a beaver pond in our forest. In any case, given the undulating topography the beavers would not be able to expand their dam or their population. Worse, Tom's tone betrayed that he had let himself be convinced by the expert.

"A beaver pond?!" I exclaimed. Forgetting about harmony and peace and abandoning my ecological ideals, I was now ranting. I wanted a forest, but a clean forest with a sparkling creek and not one with stagnant waters and trees lying around every which way and across the creek. I had no use for shavings all over the forest floor to absorb our footsteps! I did not pay top dollar for a beaver pond! I had bought a forested place, not exactly pine and birch (the birches in the area were all dead anyhow, infested with beetles after an earlier drought), but at least with spruces, a few pines, and aspens.

But that was also the rub: the beavers' favorite diet happened to be aspen. Hence their presence in such great numbers. Still, I refused to give up. If Tom was a coward, I would take care of it. Obviously, it was just too much work for Jim. He did not want to go all the way into the woods. He would have trapped them if the pond were nearer the cabin. He was just plain lazy.

Still reeling, I poured myself a sip of bourbon, as I liked to do in the wilderness. It made me feel tough, like one of the trappers or lumberjacks whose empty bottles—silent witnesses of earlier, more heroic times—I collected in the forest and in back of our two cabins. Whiskey and aspirin! If the beaver saga was allowed to go on, would they become my diet, too?

Strange Bedfellows

WITH THE ARRIVAL OF WINTER, snow and ice covered the ground and erased the beaver tracks, at least temporarily, from our memory. After Christmas, snow had begun to fall again and the thermometer suddenly dropped to a steady twenty below for close to a month. Sometime in February, we hiked in on another moonlit night with our familiar Duluth pack, sinking into the snow, struggling with balance—we had yet to acquire snowshoes—and, to assuage our misery, congratulating ourselves for at least no longer having our "loaner cat," Doreen, with us.

Doreen was a rather high-strung and neurotic feline that we had been boarding the previous year. Our old cat, Jo, had died a couple of winters before. In fact, sadly, she died on a cold January night at the cabin. She passed away three months short of her twentieth birthday, and her loss was heartfelt. Jo had been a faithful companion during all our travels and travails; she shepherded the children as they grew from infancy to adolescence; she had shared all our joys and sorrows. She had been along on all our early camping adventures and, during those last years, was enjoying not only encounters with bears but also, we liked to think, the sudden "comfort" afforded by real cabins instead of the tents. She followed us around everywhere—out to the shed, the outhouse, the swimming rock, and even up the path through the forest to the spring. She liked to prowl around in pursuit of mice, chipmunks, birds, or whatever crossed her path, though given her advanced age, she was seldom successful in her hunt.

The summer following Jo's death, our daughter thought we should overcome our mourning by temporarily housing a cat whose owner was leaving the country for a while and had worked herself into a "state" at the thought of having to resort to euthanasia if she could not find an appropriate sitter. We were not too open to the idea, but eventually, as it always seemed to go, threats of having to put the animal to sleep appealed to our sentimental side, and two days later, Doreen arrived in her pet taxi.

Our old cat had been a simple calico. This one, however, was almost pedigreed. She had long brown silky hair and was fully conscious of her lineage and her beauty. She arrived complete with basket, playpen, brush, pills, suppositories, vitamins, and even a paste to lick from a tube to get rid of hair balls. And Doreen demanded constant attention. She knew when it was time for her brushing. She called me to her scratching post, perched herself on top, and stuck out her head to be petted. She knew when it was time for her paste. She ate a quarter of a can of wet food a day at an appointed hour and then needed to have her teeth groomed. We decided to simplify her regimen, but the cat resisted. She enjoyed all the fuss and was not favorably disposed toward shortcuts. Doreen was as pretty as she was neurotic and got her feelings hurt for a trifle. But she was a good huntress. In our city house, she was vicious with mice and birds. She found mice in the house that we never even knew existed. Our old cat must have just kept a peaceful coexistence with them for many years.

Given her instincts as a huntress, we thought Doreen would love the cabin and the forest. We were not entirely wrong, but she hated to travel by car, and each time, mewed her heart out during the entire trip. Once we had arrived, she did like to hunt and made a serious dent in the mouse and vole population that had been thriving on the never diminishing supply of nuts, bird seed, and flour. But there was another side to Doreen's enjoyment of the country. She discovered mosquitoes, and she hated them.

The density of the mosquito population depended on the season and the weather. This particular year, the year of Doreen, an earlier drought was followed by a wet, humid summer that caused a lot of floods in the area. The clay ground was so saturated with rainwater that it seemed spongy. Rivulets formed, and on a particularly bad day, the water rushed under our cabins and even came up through the floor of the upper cabin. People everywhere were complaining. Rain and high water levels were the topic of conversation that summer at local taverns and on the porch of the Rondeaus' log building that housed the store and, by now, Jim's "gallery." Mosquito jokes abounded: "Only six inches of snow'll kill them!" As it turned out, even that prediction was wrong. When we went skiing later on around Thanksgiving, I pushed my pole into the snow and out flew a mosquito.

Doreen's loathing for mosquitoes was instant and everlasting. When she arrived at the cabin she gradually overcame her initial fear of the outside, and after a long while she wandered up to the front door, where she stationed herself and peered out through the screen. She was squinting intently at the action at the bird feeder. Soon a light buzz was heard in the air. A mosquito gracefully flew down and landed right on Doreen's nose. There it did what its instincts taught it to do. Doreen bolted. She flew through the cabin, into the bedroom, and disappeared under the bed before she emerged several hours later. After this initial debacle the incident was repeated several times.

Never would Doreen get used to the insects. Every time one approached and landed on her neck, her back, or—oh, horror— as that first time, on her nose, Doreen made a dash to get under the bed. There she crouched for a long time before venturing out again. She sat in the folds of the big green Duluth pack stored there. "Doreen has gone back to Duluth," Tom liked to joke. Doreen's enjoyment of the North Woods was seriously curtailed by her categorical dislike of mosquitoes, though not quite enough to make her give up hunting entirely.

Doreen remained a first-rate huntress. She demanded to go out at night, around ten o'clock, after it was dark and the mosquitoes, whose ferocious hour was at dusk, had finally calmed down a bit. So Doreen ventured out late at night and did not return until the wee hours, at which time she would jump up on an overturned barrel next to our bedroom window and scratch at the screen until someone got up to let her in. There was nothing unusual one night when, once again, Doreen asked to be let in. Tom stumbled out in the dark and opened the door. Doreen came trotting into the bedroom. She seemed in a happy disposition—so much the better. It was a rare thing and we were able to appreciate it, since she spent so much daytime moping under the bed.

Doreen usually slept between us, but one night, after demanding to be let in, she had more trouble than usual settling down. After she jumped up on the bed I was waiting for her to get still and go to sleep. But she kept rooting around. I waited some more. Still the cat was agitated. Suddenly a thought crossed my mind. Tom, who was also unable to sleep, must have had the same thought. He turned on his flashlight and shone it right on Doreen, sitting between us. There on the bed was a mouse. It was not quite dead, though it had been seriously mauled. It was lying on its back, sticking its paws in the air as if imploring us for help. Doreen, her yellow eyes glowing in the light, was proud of herself and wanted to be praised. "The goddamned cat has put a mouse in our bed," Tom's words broke the silence of the night. The mouse stirred, and Doreen crouched and pounced on it. The mouse squealed. I screamed. A commotion followed. The light went out. I heard Tom grappling for the flashlight. He finally found it. The mouse was still there, on the crumpled sheets in the space between us. "Get out of here!" Tom shouted. The bewildered cat ran to the door, with Tom not far behind her, swinging the by now dead mouse by its tail. He threw the mouse out the door, and the cat ran after it in the dark.

She must have found her prey, because all became eerily quiet out there in the thick of night.

Back in the cabin, our nervous tension finally broke. The mouse was gone. We climbed back under our feather comforter and began to laugh. Soon we were roaring. After a minute we were even howling, slapping our thighs while recounting to each other how we had found out about the mouse. Funny how a tiny animal could create such commotion. From then on, every time Doreen climbed into bed with us, we were suspicious. I held my breath and listened for strange noises. It was only once she had calmed down and I could hear her regular breathing that I was able to drift off to sleep.

The mouse incident did not repeat itself. From then on, Doreen displayed her trophies on the doorstep. We duly praised her for her exploits, and she felt flattered. She loved her hunting expeditions, though she never quite got used to life in the woods because of the mosquitoes. At the end of the season, she was probably happy to go. Doreen left in early October, when her owner returned and was ready to resume doting on her. They both seemed truly excited at finding each other again.

Once in the cabin, we continued to reminisce about Doreen and the mouse while busying ourselves with the lamps and the stove. Soon the thermometer, which hung five feet above the floor, was climbing steadily. The objects down below were still cold and would take time to absorb heat. The flannel sheets, which always felt ice cold initially, would gradually warm under the contact of our bodies. I was the first to call it a night. At least, I joked one more time, Doreen isn't here to put mice in our bed. I got ready to tuck in, and, in the semidarkness of the room, lit only by the reflection of the oil lamp and the flickering of the fire in the next room, I pulled back and climbed under the covers that—in defiance of Louise's orders—we no longer packed away for the winter.

I nestled into the soft burgundy flannel sheets, laid my head on the comfortable pillow, and pushed one hand under it. It touched something fuzzy. A split second. Then a thought: a foreign object.

What was it? Something unfamiliar and furry. It didn't even move. I screamed. I yanked my hand back, scrambled out from under the sheets, and jumped out of the bed. Tom came to the rescue with a lamp. I was shaking. Gently, we lifted the pillow. Underneath, there was a flat something that still had the recognizable shape of an animal. We looked closer and shivered at the sight. It looked like the flattened outline of a squirrel, of which there was only some fur left. A row of teeth lay neatly arranged against the background of the flannel. The rest had disintegrated. It had been freeze-dried, as Tom, never at a loss for words, was quick to declare.

The animal, most likely a squirrel, must have burrowed into the cabin and was perhaps unable to escape, we conjectured, unless it had been killed by a predator, possibly one of our earlier visitors, a weasel. The animal's carcass had slowly rotted and made a hole in the brand-new L.L. Bean sheets. I removed the bedding and, shivering, put on the thin summer sheets, already missing the experience of the pleasure and warmth of our lovely flannel. Maybe Louise had been right after all.

By the time the commotion was over and things had gotten back to "normal," I was wide awake. I went back to the other room and made myself some herbal tea, to which I added a spoonful of honey and some bourbon. Warming my hands over the cup, I slowly rocked myself in our green wicker chair and laughed with Tom about unexpected turns of events in the North Woods.

Tree Nailing

ON SEVERAL CROSS-COUNTRY SKIING EXPEDITIONS later that month, we had decided to go in the direction of the beaver pond. Winter, we somehow assumed, forgetting about the carved trees and wood shavings we saw on our land earlier, would be a time of truce in the beaver war. Wrong. Our sorties revealed that there were many more "beaver trees" than in the previous summer. Subzero temperatures and a thick layer of ice had not prevented the squatters from continuing their labor. From then on, as had our summer outings, all our skiing trips too painfully led us to the growing "disaster area," as we came to call it. We were drawn there as if by a magnet. My faith in Jim Rondeau was shattered. How could he have told us the beavers were not going to expand, I cried out, while vainly trying to get one ski over a snow-covered log, a rather treacherous affair because of the unpredictable holes hidden by the snow. How could we make them move?

Our obsession intensified. My ecological principles, not to mention my vision of nature, were ever more gravely compromised. In no way had my bookish knowledge prepared me for this real-life situation. Beavers were destroying our trees—and for what? Where was my longed for harmony? I had not foreseen such dilemmas. Instead of taking meditative hikes or skiing in the forest as I had imagined, we now scheduled daily visits to the beaver pond. Summer and now even winter, we seemed to spend all of our time running after beavers.

One sleepless night, I had an idea. Rob had protected the mature aspen trees along the river by wrapping chicken wire around the base of their trunks. Clearly, the beavers did not like to chew on metal surfaces. Why couldn't we do the same in the forest? We would cut off the beavers' food supply and they would have to move, I informed Tom over breakfast. A brilliant idea, he acknowledged.

Winter lingered, and in March there was still enough snow cover in the woods that we could ski out to the pond with rolls of chicken wire. The wire was heavy, and we could transport only one roll at a time on an old-fashioned sled we had found in the shed. We went to the pond equipped with wire, nails, and a hammer. Tom even wore a carpenter's apron he had inherited from Rob. "The perfect outfit for a sunny winter day in the wilderness," I sneered. We started with several large aspens, some of which had already been gnawed and were starting to show the characteristic hourglass shape. We pounded our hands as often as we did the heads of the nails, and we alternately laughed and swore, depending on whose fingers the hammer hit.

The supply of chicken wire was quickly exhausted, and neither of us felt ready to go several miles to replenish the stock. Why not just put large nails into the trees at the height where the beavers stood up against the trees? That way, they wouldn't be able to lean on the trunks and would be even less able to chew, I suggested. Another brilliant idea. We worked away for several hours, nailing tree after tree, deciding which one to do first, which one was larger than the other, which one more accessible. After a while, all the remaining aspens and ashes round the pond were safely "spiked." Ha! Now the beavers would move.

When, after another week or two, we returned to inspect the fruits of our labor, we were once again stunned. Since all the trees around the pond had either been felled, wired, or nailed, the beavers had shifted their attention to those on the hill at the back of the pond. They used the first tree as a bridge to the next and kept out of the snow. They had set up shop in an area where the trees, mainly aspen and ash, were smaller and more tender. It did not take them as long to chew through them. The devastation was even more overwhelming. Trees and shavings were everywhere. For a moment, all we could do was gape. Then I blew. I had not, I repeated over and over, bought a beaver pond. I had paid top dollar, a point on which I liked to insist, for a forest. If, at least, the beavers were sensible—if only they ate one tree at a time. But no, they had to start on all of them together and nibble on one branch here, one leaf there. In the meantime, we were left with a seemingly expanding battlefield. More action was definitely needed here to ensure my vision of wilderness. We hauled in another supply of nails, all set to "spike" every tree in sight that was still standing. I was all set to nail the entire forest if necessary. It was, we felt, a humane and polite way to tell the beavers to move, and would protect the trees and also our investment.

The next day was bright and sunny. Instead of going out for some fun skiing, we floundered back to the beaver pond. Tom wore his apron and carried the little bag from the lumberyard with all the supplies that we now kept on hand. One by one we began nailing the young trees. It was, once again, a tough job. I handed the nails to Tom, who hammered them into the trees. We couldn't handle the nails with gloves on, and in March it was still cold enough for our fingers to freeze quickly. We spent the entire day at it, and as dusk began closing in on us, we still had a stand of trees to go. Wearily, we skied back to the cabin. "And what did you do over your spring break," I said sarcastically. "I went tree nailing!" People would think we were crazy, and they would probably be right.

Every morning, for the next three or four days, we headed straight for the beaver pond. How many times we actually hit our fingers instead of the nails was not documented. Every evening, when we arrived back at the cabin, I headed straight for the bourbon.

Nature Attacks

SPRING CAME EARLY THAT YEAR. the river opened, and once again it was time for the annual tree planting ceremony that continued to combine so much pleasure and pain. We persevered in our plan to diversify our forest and discourage the beaver along the river and around the field. Tom, braving the mosquitoes and the blackflies, even ventured out to the beaver pond to do some replanting along its shores. When we inspected the result of our hard labor a few weeks later, the seedlings looked quite healthy. Indeed, their survival rate seemed to be more than about two out of three, a good ratio in nature where, despite rumors of abundance, survival was an achievement. As we were scrupulously inspecting the various planting sites—except those with the tamaracks, which by now were so overgrown with brush that they were no longer detectable—we discovered a kind of white cocoon on several bushes as well as on the branches of the smaller aspens. Some of the trees even had a few dark caterpillars on them, hanging from the branches or feeling their way along with their wavy forward movements. Where had these things come from? There were too many to dismiss them as isolated occurrences. I had a bad feeling. Tom, forever the optimist, tried to dismiss it. "Oh, no," he said soothingly, "those are just a few spring insects. They'll go away."

Later that day, while shopping in the neighboring town, we bought a copy of the local newspaper. There, right on the front page, we saw a picture of one of these fuzzy creatures. "Tent Caterpillar Attack!" the headlines read in big bold letters. The article truly made it sound like an impending plague. The caterpillars, I quickly learned, emerged in great numbers every seventeen years, and in between, remained passive. That was without a doubt, I speculated, why Rob and Louise, who had owned our place for fifteen years between episodes, had never mentioned them.

I pored over the article. Our area, I read out loud, was being invaded by tent caterpillars that came in great numbers and, while harmless to humans, attacked trees—especially aspens, but also others and even bushes—by eating the leaves. The trees had to grow new leaves twice in the same season and were considerably weakened in the process. Caterpillars came in cycles, and this year looked like the first of a three-year cycle. All areas were not hit to the same degree. With unabated optimism and, apparently without having learned his lesson from the beavers, Tom retorted that surely, our place would be spared.

He was wrong. A few weeks later we came back with my mother to celebrate her eightieth birthday. It was a special occasion, and we had driven up to the cabin with the matriarch sitting in the back of the car and commenting on everything, from the looks of cars to people's driving and the "monotonous" scenery along the highway. When we drove down the road to the gate, the tall aspens that lined the road and whose branches touched to form a cathedral-like roof looked rather bare. Were the leaves not out yet in this part of the forest in early June? we wondered.

When we got out of the car we at once noticed a strange dripping sound. Yet there wasn't a cloud in the sky, and it clearly wasn't raining. Then reality hit: there were hordes of caterpillars crawling everywhere. They were climbing up tree trunks and hanging from branches. They were clinging to leaves. What we had thought was water dripping was caterpillars dropping to the ground. Wherever we looked, there they were. Not only had the leaves been eaten, the cabins, covered with white cocoons, looked like enchanted cottages in a fairy tale. We tried to walk around, but it quickly became obvious that we had to avoid wooded areas if we did not want the caterpillars falling into our hair and all over our bodies. For the next few days it continued to "rain" caterpillars. Getting to the outhouse was an adventure. Before leaving the cabin we put our sweatshirts on with the hoods tight around our faces. And when we returned we imitated the ancient ritual of "delousing," which we transformed into "decaterpillaring" each other.

Against our expectations, my mother turned out to be the most accepting. "Oh, yes," she said, "I have seen it all before—one year in Provence, in the south of France. That was the year your dad wanted me to come along on a painting expedition. I wore a broad-brimmed hat to protect myself, but Henry had to give up painting his landscapes. The caterpillars kept falling on his wet paint!" She laughed, recalling the scene. "But this is not the south of France," I retorted in despair. My mother, unperturbed and pragmatic, inquired, "How often do they come?" "Every seventeen years, we've been told." "Well," she said, "you better sell the place before the next seventeen years." Her humor was not immediately appreciated. We were too much immersed in our predicament. It was impossible to walk anywhere under or near trees. Trying to sit out in a lawn chair promised to be equally treacherous. The grass was crawling with caterpillars. As soon as one of us sat down, they began their steady, unstoppable climb up one's legs, pants, socks, or whatever surface was available for them to hold on to.

I had a bright idea. Rob and Louise had left us a large screened tent in which they liked to sit on hot summer days to "catch the breeze." The screen also kept insects out. So why not put it up now, though it was not quite the season? The caterpillars would be unable to enter it. We all agreed. After fetching the tent, Tom and I busied ourselves with the practical aspects while my mother supervised. It was an old-fashioned tent, and we had to work hard to drive the wooden stakes into the ground, which was still rather hard. We managed, at last, to get the frame together and were now trying to put on the canvas. At first all went smoothly. We began to see the shape of a tent, and only the last pole, the middle one in front, which was also the one that held up the entire structure, was left. We had to raise the tent, hook one end of the pole to the roof and ram the other end into the ground. But that final result continued to elude us.

We were already on our third try, and each time, the structure collapsed. In growing frustration, Tom announced he would do it alone and curtly asked me to step aside. My mother and I watched from the sideline as Tom balanced the pole and pushed hard. Up went the tent, then up, another push, and the pole seemed secure. Tom let go, and no sooner had he taken his hands off the pole than down came the whole thing, but this time he was trapped inside.

For a brief moment, total silence reigned. There was only a flat piece of green canvas on the ground with a big bulge at one end. Then the bulge began to move. At that point my nervous tension turned into laughter and soon I was roaring. Tom, still inside his trap, began to growl. He was not amused. But he looked so funny, I protested. My mother, displaying her wisdom acquired with age, gestured to me with ever bigger eyes. To no avail. I could not stop laughing. Tom's anger grew as he tried to extricate himself from canvas, poles, ropes, and the wretched caterpillars that, unperturbed by the commotion, had started again on their steady climb! The episode ended with Tom directing his anger against the unsuspecting crowd of caterpillars. The tent never stood upright, and we finally had to seek refuge inside the cabin. The caterpillars had won the battle and the war.

Later in the season, the next big thrill was to pick off all the silk webs from the cabin walls. We had been in no hurry to do so, but pressure from what we imagined to be the critical eye of the inspector of the North Woods was mounting even though no one could see our cabins. When we ventured out, people in the community wondered how we were coping with the cocoons. They kept on asking, until Tom and I provided the proper answer and, to keep our promise, felt obligated to get down to business. The white splotches were everywhere—on the logs, between the logs, under the shingles, in every nook and cranny we could find. It took days to get them off. To make the activity less tedious, we listened to baseball on the portable radio. By the end of the cleanup I knew everything about the game, even every team's lineup. This was the one aspect Tom felt to be a positive result of the tent caterpillars.

The caterpillars were around for an entire month and then turned into moths that would return the following year. The aspens were stripped. They had to grow new leaves in the same season, which sapped their strength and made them vulnerable. The caterpillars came back the next year and the year after. The second and third years were not as calamitous as the first. The plague had left its mark, though: many of the aspens were dying, and bald spots were visible everywhere in the forest. Was this the promised harmony?

The First Trapper

Tent caterpillars, swimming, hiking, canoeing, fishing, mushrooming, and the excitement of observing birds had made us forget, at least temporarily, about the beavers. The forest was extremely dense that year, and the thought of fighting our way through thick brush armed with the ax and mosquito repellent, stumbling over downed trees and limbs, and scratching our faces and arms until they were bloody had lost a great deal of its original appeal. It was quite unexpected, then, that one day in August we received a call from an elderly man with a heavy northern Minnesota accent. He introduced himself as Dale Kostad and said that someone from the Department of Natural Resources had informed him we had problems with beavers and might be looking for a trapper. And yaah (he drew out the vowel), he would be willing to come over the next day to inspect the situation. Although we had repressed the thought of our beaver plight since our tree nailing, a detail that I at least was hesitant to let the trapper see for fear of ridicule ("Heard about those people who nailed all their trees?" I could only imagine how he would tell it to a community roaring with laughter), it seemed wise to have the site inspected and so we readily agreed to the man's offer.

Around ten-thirty the following morning we heard the coughing sound of an engine. We put down our coffee cups and quickly walked up the hill to the parking knoll to investigate. Dale puttered up the road in his little green pickup truck. He parked at the top of the hill and slowly emerged from the cab with a broad grin under his drab olive fisherman's hat. "So pleased to meet you," he uttered, with the funny Scandinavian *o* particular to the region and that, in his dialect, was particularly strong. We suppressed a smile, introduced ourselves, and proceeded to escort Dale down the path to the lower cabin.

We made rather slow progress. Our possible trapper paused here and there, commenting on plants and various tracks, holding forth about weather conditions, mosquitoes, deer, tent caterpillars, and other everyday topics. It turned out that he was quite a talker. In his mid-seventies and in good physical shape, owing perhaps −99− to his moderate lifestyle and excellent genes, Dale was knowledgeable in all aspects of life. In fact, he had a comment to make on everything.

Tom ushered him through the front door, and Dale sat down at the table on the porch. "Would you like a cup of coffee?" Tom inquired politely. This offer was the custom of the area, and jokes abounded about the visit of two northern Minnesotans who sat silently over coffee. When the visitor finally left after a good hour or so of total quiet, he told his host, "Thanks, Ole, I had a great time!" This trait, however, was not shared by Dale, who was a genuine mill of words.

He inquired about his "hosts," our presence here in his native country, and when that subject was exhausted, he launched into a lengthy narrative concerning his own childhood and youth in the region. He was not unpleasant to listen to, and the details about his parents' homestead and the hardships of cutting wood, heating water, cooking, canning, and hunting in his youth had us on the edge of our seats. But I, at last, less tolerant than Tom, felt that time was ticking away and we were not really getting to our topic.

In no apparent hurry, Dale had, by now, become theoretical. He looked at the original outside wall of our antique log cabin, which was currently enclosed with a new porch. That wall, consisting of hand-hewn logs, had been patiently restored by our predecessors and was our pride and joy. The areas between the logs were filled in with a kind of concrete that had been handcolored light brown. It had the look of an old log cabin, the kind that is commonly featured on the covers of magazines specializing in "country living." But Dale's point of view on the topic was quite different. He focused his sharp eye on the logs, which provided the occasion for a lecture. No, those logs are not well put together, was his opening remark. Tom's curiosity was piqued. I was vexed. No, Dale added, a Finn would never do it this way. And since he, Dale, was part Finnish, a heavy value judgment was implicit in these remarks.

A Finn, Dale said, cuts the logs so that they don't crack like these. Finns make a deep incision along the length of a log so that it will fit snugly on its neighbor below. The slit also allowed the wood to contract without harming the material, such as putty, cement, or strips of wood, placed at the juncture.

Tom seemed genuinely interested in the shapes of logs. I stationed myself behind Dale so that he could not see me and began rolling my eyes, both in the direction of the beaver lodge and at my wristwatch. Tom pretended to ignore my ever wilder gestures. He kept his attention focused on Dale and smiled patiently. Did Tom really care, or was he just putting Dale on? As was often the case, I couldn't tell. Tom's patience could be exasperating.

Dale continued, unperturbed. From logs he had moved on to bees. I had reached the boiling point. Smiling, Tom finally acknowledged my suffering by moving one hand, a kind of baseball signal meant to make me "cool down." Yes, Dale could be heard saying by now, "The bees . . . do you like honey?" He let Tom pour him another cup of coffee and reached for the sugar. I watched him sink a big spoonful into the dark brew. "Good coffee," Dale declared approvingly, underlining each word with a nod of his head. "Yes, I had bees, bees," he said wistfully, "and they made a honey like you never tasted before . . ."

"What about the beavers?" I finally exploded. "The beeeeavers—when are you coming to get them?" "Oh!" Dale was startled. He seemed to wake from a dream. "Oh, yes, the beavers," Tom said, finally giving me a little support. "Oh, yes, where are they?" Tom pointed toward the lodge near the cabin. "Here is one house, but there's another, in the woods in the back of the field, and that's where something really has to be done." "They've destroyed our favorite area," I interjected, encouraged by Tom's sudden involvement. "Well," Tom said, "maybe we should walk out there." Dale was obviously more interested in talking about bees and sweetening his coffee than in taking a hike in the woods. Reluctantly, probably to save face, he agreed, and we all went into the woods to review the situation.

Dale was one of a kind. The walk took twice the usual time. We –101– stopped at every plant and tree so that he could comment on it. Even though he was in really good shape, it was not all that easy for him to reach the remote area. He liked walking on groomed paths and was not up for climbing over fallen logs and hacking through seven-foot brush. Nonetheless, we made it. All was still at the beaver pond. There was no sign of life. The needles of uncut submerged trees had turned rusty and were falling off. Toppled aspens were everywhere. Other trees were still standing, though most looked like hourglasses toward the bottom. The once serene place with the running creek was a muddy mess. The lodge was covered with moss, and grass was growing from it. There were no new branches lying on top. Dale poked around, inspected, thought a bit, inspected again. "There are no beavers in here," was his verdict, at last. "No, there aren't any beavers in here." "Well, where have they gone?" I asked, impatiently. He did not know, but added that they must have died. "Beavers die, yes, they die. They catch a disease and then the whole lodge dies out. That's what must have happened. They died."

Thus concluded the beaver tour for Dale. "There are no beavers here," he could be heard muttering on our way back. "No, no beavers." And in any event, he added (perhaps because he sensed that the coffee and sugar source had dried up), he would not be able to take care of them. He was now a snowbird; that is, he went south for the winter, to Florida. He was up here only between May and September, and beaver season did not start until the end of October. Beavers had to grow their winter coats before they could be trapped, or they wouldn't be worth anything.

But that wasn't the point, I objected. By now, I felt that we had been had. Dale had spent a good two hours with us, knowing he would not be able to do the job. What was the point of his visit, anyhow? And I was suspicious of his evaluation that the beavers had died. In the spring, when we had done all the tree nailing, it was obvious that they were thriving. Dale was firm in his assessment. We walked in silence. At least, Tom did not invite Dale back to the cabin, which undoubtedly he would have accepted despite his fall from grace. He ushered the retired trapper to his truck and saw him off.

I was muttering about ineptitude, imposition, and wasted time. Only the approaching noon hour, with its promise of a sun-drenched swim in the clear waters under a deep blue sky could calm me down.

A New Beaver Dam

WITH HIS UNSHAKABLE FAITH IN HUMANITY, Tom readily accepted Dale's verdict. The beavers were gone; they might even have been wiped out by disease, poor things. Tom was ready to groom the area by clearing it of debris, opening the dam, and replanting. He was eager for us to "get on with our lives," as they say on the news after every major catastrophe. The more resistant of the two, I grudgingly trotted along with him, across the field and through the forest to our most familiar spot. An overwhelming calm greeted us there. But then, it *was* the middle of the afternoon, and the beavers were nocturnal. I looked around at the massacre: trees lying across the creek, on top of each other, in the pond. The few that had been disdained by the beavers' delicate palates stood helpless in several feet of water, their branches stretching upward as if imploring an unresponsive heaven for a better fate.

There was no time to waste, Tom admonished. We must get to work. First, we would open the dam to empty the pond; then we would saw up some of the trees; and in a few weeks, when the ground was colder, we could even do a little fall planting. The survival rate for trees planted in the fall was not as good as in spring, but many did make it through the winter. Tom, wearing his blue overalls to protect against the ubiquitous mosquitoes, took out his large ax and began hacking at the dam.

The structure was amazingly tough. We could never help marveling at the beavers' undeniable talents when we inspected the powerful mass of clay, large branches, fresh twigs, and rocks. Once again we worked up a sweat, warded off mosquitoes and flies, strained our backs, and sank into clay and water. After almost an hour, the water flowed freely, and the level of the pond quickly dropped.

The creek had its little waterfall back. It opened up into a miniature sandy delta, before narrowing and dropping off rapidly through some mossy rocks and boulders before eventually emptying into the river. Just beyond the sandy area, an ash grove with young, bright green trees had caught our attention, and Tom suggested we hike down to take a look at it. Perhaps we could follow the creek all the way to its end, I suggested. We had done a day's work and could return with our chainsaw to finish cleaning up on another day, after the pond had had a chance to drain.

We gingerly climbed over fallen trees, slipped on slick rocks, and stepped into the deep holes along the water's edge that signaled beaver tunnels and that were now hidden by tall grass. Buoyed by success, we felt neither our wet feet nor our sore ankles. We proudly looked back up at the hole in the dam and the waterfall we had restored. Savoring our victory, we followed the swiftly moving creek for a couple hundred yards, and then thought we noticed a change in its flow. Could it be an illusion? The creek was flattening out at this point and therefore was slower. The unexpected stillness of the water revived recent unpleasant memories. We picked up our pace. Suddenly—a tree with an hourglass shape. Then shavings and more half-chewed trees. The beavers! They were living downstream since we had nailed their upper territory.

Our hearts sank. What were we going to do *this* time? We could not nail an entire forest, hoping the beavers would migrate back down to the river and live happily, miles away from us. Why were they so determined to live in *my* forest? Deaf to Tom's feeble remarks that that this was, after all, wilderness, I protested louder than ever. We were by now almost running alongside the placid creek, trying to find the cause of its stagnation. We stumbled and fell, adding a few more bloody scratches from thorny branches, but nothing could stop our quest.

Finally, we arrived at the ash grove, the goal of our hike, and what did we see: a brand-new beaver pond with a dam at least twice the length of the old one. A dam! I exclaimed, adding a few expletives. It was right at the edge of the ash grove, and the young trees were already standing in water, soon to join the others in premature death. Through the branches, in the afternoon sun, we could even make out a spanking-new lodge. The beavers had not died out, they had simply moved.

We had been tricked, and all our work had been for nothing. Breaking the dam above had even helped because it pumped fresh water into the area below. Yes, I knew all the arguments in favor of dams: they benefited fish and other animals. Ducks liked to nest near them; countless water bugs and aquatic plants would provide food for wildlife. They controlled flooding and helped fertilize the soil. And yes, I knew that American civilization could not have been built without the help of the beavers. By now, I was even ready to concede that "order" in nature included droughts, tent caterpillars, and beaver ponds. But I had not bargained for and did not want that kind of order. I wanted what we had bought: little creeks and pristine forest in which I could commune with nature, not be at war with it.

I was livid, but Tom took it in stride. We had worked all afternoon only to help the beavers settle into their new spot! We climbed over several more fallen logs, through thick brush, and were finally able to get onto the new dam. Halfheartedly, we decided to try our luck once more. Tom took out his ax and made a chink. Like a tightrope walker, he advanced to the middle of the dam, trying to avoid falling. He hacked a second hole in the middle. The water began to flow, and the new pond was beginning to empty. How long would it take? It was already late in the afternoon. In an hour or so, the beavers would wake up and come out to repair their new dam. If the water ran out too quickly, they would wake up even earlier and hurry out here. We strained our eyes but could not see the familiar shape in the water. When the beavers came up to look at you and floated in the water with only their eyes and ears visible, they were so perfectly camouflaged that it gave one a jolt when, suddenly, a "stick" turned into a tail-slapping beaver, ready to dive.

At the moment, nothing stirred in the receding water. How long would it take after we left before an army of furry engineers swam out and orchestrated a repair session? My murderous thoughts came back once more. The beavers simply had to go. But how? Dynamite works best, one of the representatives of the DNR had said. That was out of the question because we would blow ourselves up. Shooting was unsavory, and, anyway, Tom had tried that and failed. We also had hoped to find a trapper, but that had not worked out either. Exhausted and at our wits' end, we hiked back to the cabin in silence. "The beavers have to go, the beavers have to go," I muttered feebly under my breath.

The Logging Letter

–107–

ANOTHER WINTER CAME AND WENT. It was a beautiful spring day in the city. The wind was gusting from the south; puffy white clouds were racing across the sky. The branches were still bare, but somehow it was clear that the long winter was really over. Soon, I pondered, not without elation, we would be driving north to our place in the woods for the annual tree-planting ceremony. Tree planting was even more of a necessity now, after the recent drought, the invasion by tent caterpillars, and the devastation by the beavers that was still unsolved. We had put in an especially large order for red pines, the only trees that, so far at least, were resistant to most plagues and scourges. Relegating flies, heat, and bodily aches to oblivion, I anticipated the moment with pleasure.

I was home alone, sipping my usual cup of coffee, lost in thought. How comforting it was to have all that land up north, in spite of the beaver problems. With the necessary distance between us, I even felt my soul expanding with sympathy for the animals, though not to the point of relinquishing my murderous plans entirely. Yet, how I loved the untouched look of the forest! Since it adjoined county and federal land, it could not be built up, and from our porch, we would always be able to see nothing but water and vast expanses of trees. We would always be able to walk or ski for miles down winding forest paths. Even if I had not quite found the longed-for harmony, and even if life in the woods seemed more like a perpetual struggle with nature, I loved those rocky ridges with their tall aspens and occasional stands of towering pines.

Still in a state of elation, I went to get the mail. From a thick stack consisting of the usual bills, advertisements, and charitable solicitations, I sorted out the only first-class letter. It was from St. Louis County. What could they be writing to us about? Had we forgotten to pay our taxes? I opened the envelope and took out a letter. Another paper fell to the floor. I glanced down and could make out a map. After picking up the paper, I noticed it was indeed a map of our property and of the adjoining land. Blue and red lines were drawn around shaded areas with exes and numbers. What did this all mean? Disquieted, I began reading the accompanying letter. Dear Mr. and Mrs. . . . We want to inform you that St. Louis County is intending to log several tracts of land, some of which border your property . . . It was signed by Ralph Kahn, "Forest Coordinator."

The words were beginning to dance in front of my eyes. I ran to the window to read the letter in full daylight. I compared it with the drawing. There was no mistake: the county was logging "some" of its land, and that land happened to border the entire eastern side of our property. All the trees where we liked to hike and ski would be gone. I was stunned. Our forest would be completely destroyed. The Forest Service's claim was that aspen had to be clear-cut to produce a healthy forest and that the trees were growing quickly. And they did. But it would take another fifty to sixty years before they would reach the same height. We most likely would not live to see it. It was in the North Woods that I had discovered mortality when I had begun to realize how long it took a tree to grow. I would fight this, but how? And Tom was not around to help. He was out on the West Coast for a couple of days. He would come home, slightly giddy from his ventures, and I would give him the bad news.

Tom returned, full of spunk. He found me distant, moody, and brooding. What was wrong? I did not have the heart to tell him right away. But finally, I blurted out the news and pointed to the letter I had conspicuously displayed on his desk, though somehow, he had until now overlooked it. As he was reading, the happy glow on his face turned crimson. He would never let this happen. How dare they cut down his forest! He was going to fight it.

The following day, we started calling official places and lawyers. We were, of course, put on hold, told to push buttons for more options, and generally referred from one place to the next. We spoke to officials in the state capital, to others in the main offices of St. Louis County, to local members of the Sierra Club, the Audubon Society, to people at the Forestry Department, and at the university. Finally, we were talking to private lawyers, whose names had been given us by the Sierra Club. Specialists in environmental matters, they were well acquainted with the laws. None seemed optimistic. Unless we could prove that our own rights had been violated, there was not much recourse. We brooded. I offered to throw myself in front of the loggers' machinery. Tom did not think this was a good idea, but in turn, he threatened to shoot them. I found his solution a bit dramatic. We would publish our story in the paper. We would raise a public outcry.

Little did we realize that our story was one of thousands. It was repeated all over the county, the state, the country, and the world. It was close to sixty years since the last harvest and massive logging operations had been planned for the North Woods. Clearing had been going on along the county road for some time now. When driving to the next town, one at times had the impression of traveling between two theatrical curtains of trees behind which massive devastation was taking place. And now, the operations were being extended to the heart of the forest everywhere. Some people were ready to protest. Others defended the cutting, especially those who worked for the big wood-product corporations. Many just plain did not care.

The "logging letter," as we came to refer to it, reinforced our sense of helplessness as citizens in the face of powerful organizations that might include those who were supposed to represent us. Tom suggested with grim determination that a form of terrorism might be the only way to save our cherished trees.

A Tour with the "Forest Coordinator"

RALPH KAHN WAS THE SPECIALIST who surveyed the forest for the county in order to decide which areas were to be cut. As St. Louis County's forest coordinator, he had composed the letter announcing the county's intention to log its land. The letter had been written with a rare fluency and even a touch of rhetoric. Clearly, Ralph was a new breed of technical expert. He was from the area but had trained on the West Coast and was well acquainted with the latest principles and methods of forest husbandry. Ralph had an ambivalent relationship with the local population, which he considered inattentive to nature and fixated on gasoline motors and noise. He too rode a snowmobile in the winter, but only because it enabled him to get quickly to remote areas. Otherwise, he was a man of distinction and had what seemed an uncommon appreciation for nature.

Ralph had offered to take us on a hike along our property line to show us exactly where, how, and why those trees would be harvested. You might be interested in having some of your forest logged at the same time, he added nonchalantly. Over my dead body, I exclaimed defiantly, after Tom relayed the suggestion to me.

Ralph arrived one morning in mid-June, accompanied by his yellow lab, Sasha, his companion on all outings. Ralph wore a cap bearing the inscription "Forestry in the Service of the Environment." I growled. "We probably differ on views on the environment" were my welcoming words, which contained a thinly disguised threat. Ralph was unperturbed. Aspen had to be cut, he patiently reiterated. Trees got sick, and clear-cutting was the only answer for a healthy aspen forest. His way of "building civilization," based on drawing a line between the healthy and the sick, smacked, I grumbled, of fascist propaganda. The argument also left little space for diversity.

We put on our hiking boots and left for our tour. The good news was that the property extended much farther than we had thought. The bad news was that the cutting was much more extensive than we had assumed it would be. Ralph justified it by showing us the diseased aspen trees that had developed several kinds of lethal fungi. The fungi looked like giant mushrooms attached to the tree trunk. Tom and I exchanged meaningful glances. It seemed that we had spent all our time nailing diseased trees to protect them from the beavers! It was an action you might expect of city people like us. And the beavers were the worthiest of creatures. They performed a service to the community. They logged diseased trees and helped bring about diversity. The unspoken in Ralph's persuasive reasoning was the absence of replanting. With the exception of a few pines, all trees—spruce, ash, birch, maple—were to be cut, and chances were that mainly aspens would grow back. From the loggers' point of view this was the desired condition. Big Timber even spoke of reducing the length of time between harvests from sixty to forty, and in some cases even down to thirty, years. The only planting discussed was that involving genetically altered aspens that would produce more pulp.

To let a forest return to conditions of diversity—on its own or helped by beavers—was estimated to take close to three hundred years. If one did not cut aspens, we were told, they would indeed fall and rot. Brush would take over. After this cycle, some pines would take hold, and slowly they would reestablish themselves. It was a long cycle, much more than any market-driven wood-product company was willing to accommodate and much more than any logger could sustain while his equipment sat rusting in the snow. So Big Timber, in harmony with the rest of the world, was intent on accelerating the logging cycles. It had perfected its pitch: clear-cutting produced healthy trees. Deer loved fresh poplar. Wolves were thriving on the increase in deer, and the beaver population reigned supreme.

Yet, there were many unaddressed factors. What about all the birds and animals that were pushed out of their habitat during the winter months, since that was when logging took place? Only when the ground was frozen could heavy equipment be brought in. Another unacknowledged issue was the disruption of fungi and other plants vital for diversity. And, of course, the removal of old trees also took away shelter and food for many animals.

This was not what interested Ralph Kahn, who turned a deaf ear to my concerns. He followed the company line, at least on −113− this topic. By now, we had reached the beaver creek and paused in front of some of our tall spruces. Ralph took out a device by which he could measure the age of a tree. "You have some old granddaddies here," he exclaimed, as the reading on the meter indicated one hundred and fifty to two hundred years. We looked up at the spruces swaying in the breeze. Near the top, I could see a few squirrels' nests and wondered what it would be like to sleep up there, rocked by the wind. When we reached the beaver pond and took in the devastation in silence, Ralph was sympathetic. He too suggested the "chink method," but our protests made him think of another solution. He knew of a trapper who could be of assistance, a retired forestry worker whose name and telephone number he gave us. From his words I could tell that Ralph liked nature. But his views of the forest were those of a technician rather than a poet. This categorized Ralph for me, and I could not be dissuaded.

I took inventory of the beaver pond. The once flowing creek seemed to have come to a halt. The water was stagnating, and all around lay the unmistakable signs of Mr. Castor, Mrs. Auric—as we had come to call them—and their offspring. Although we had just been assured by Ralph that beaver cut down "diseased" trees, it still broke our hearts that dozens of aspens were toppled for the sake of a few twiggy branches per tree.

The area around the new beaver house extended as far as we could see. A few ducks were already swimming in the backed-up water. As our daughter kept reminding us, the pond *was* a source of regeneration. But not on our land! I protested, forgetting about the ecological principles I had just invoked. The beavers had to go. I would contact the trapper.

Our tour concluded with a quick cup of coffee over which Ralph informed us that the cutting would most likely not begin until the following winter. Ralph did not linger with us: as a technical expert, he did not consider himself part of the local ecosystem.

Amos, the Eco-Trapper

Later that day, at my insistence, Tom called Amos, the trapper Ralph had suggested. The telephone rang for a long time, and no answering machine kicked in. It took several days of persistence before a woman's voice with a heavy regional accent finally answered. It was Edna, Amos's wife, who informed us that her husband was out "on a mission." The expression was a euphemism for the preparation of some kind of hunting trip. Amos was retired after forty years with the U.S. Forest Service and knew the North Woods well. He supplemented his meager pension by organizing hunting expeditions for city folks. Helped by his wife, Amos also hunted for sustenance. The couple knew and respected animals, but harvested them for food. Tom explained our plight and was assured that "the husband" would take care of it. Amos eventually returned our call and promised action.

On a hot summer afternoon, Amos appeared at our place in his rattling pickup truck, a composite of many different models and junkyard runs. Amos was a stocky man in his early sixties. He was physically fit, a departure from the local norm. He did not smoke and he drank little. His entire life had been spent in the woods, which he knew "like his pocket." That was, however, an inadequate expression. Rather, he was like a character out of an earlier century. He read nature like the book of God. The forest was his temple, he liked to say. He was no Sigurd Olson, though, and clearly had a more pragmatic approach to nature.

Amos wore his hair cropped short, in a flat top whose stylishness was completely unbeknownst to him. His brown uniform, after many years of service, was shiny and threadbare along the legs and seat. He carried a pocketknife on the left side of his belt and, to my astonishment, a handgun on the right. He introduced himself in his husky voice with a distinctly local inflection and, upon seeing my puzzled look, explained the presence of the weapon. It was to defend himself against the environmentalists. I was aghast. His remark, I felt, was directed at me. Yes, Amos went on, in New York State, some trappers had been shot by animal rightists, some city dwellers who knew nothing about animals or

plants. I kept silent.

Amos gladly accepted Tom's friendly offer of a cup of coffee, but he was less inclined to tell stories than he was to learn about our woods. "Yeah," he said wistfully, "it looks real thick, real thick in there. Have you spotted any mountain lions?" My eyes became wider by the minute. "Or coyote?" he continued, unperturbed. Not since my childhood stories about the American West had I heard the word. "There must be some in there," Amos continued, disregarding Tom's negative answers. Tom tried to reaffirm that our primary interest was beavers, but Amos was insistent. Had we been hunting? Were there many deer? No, Tom explained, and added that he occasionally went with a male party to another site, but that he was interested in recruiting me to hunt on our property this year. I could not believe my ears. Hunting here, he went on, would be a way of getting to know our land.

Amos finally asked Tom to show him the beaver sites, and the men took off. I watched them walk down the first slope. They paused to discuss the closest beaver house, as I could tell from their gestures, before crossing the field and disappearing into the forest.

It was a long time before they reappeared. They stopped on their way back, and I could see Amos pointing to various plants that I could not make out from where I stood. The two parted in front of the cabin. Amos was not one to hang around. Tom opened the door and entered, beaming. "Never have I learned so much," he announced. Tom was prone to exaggeration, but this time he didn't seem to be overstating things. He was backing up his assessment with facts and details. He was amazed by Amos's knowledge of nature. In just an hour, he had shown Tom wild hops, medicinal herbs, chokecherries, highbush cranberries, and juniper berries with which to make jellies, as well as edible roots. I was a little unsettled by the sudden prospect of digging for roots, boiling leaves, canning more berries. The forest had an abundance of nourishment. Amos had also shown him mountain lion and coyote tracks, right on our land! Tom's excitement was without bounds. In addition, the trapper had shown him some good hunting spots and promised to come back in a few days to help us set up a couple of deer stands, one for him and one for me. I saw that Tom was speaking in earnest.

Edna, the Woodswoman

THE FOLLOWING SUNDAY, AMOS RETURNED WITH HIS WIFE. Sexism did not exist with folks up here: that was an invention of city dwellers. On a farm or in the woods, all hands were required. The women still oversaw the household and did the accounting where needed. As in the old days, men roamed the woods. Women stayed closer to home and tended to the garden and the house. Only occasionally, as in the case of hunting, did women leave the hearth.

When Amos and Edna visited us that Sunday, they had just had their weekly treat, which consisted of breakfast at their favorite coffee shop in the nearest town. Edna was tall and bony. She looked as strong as an ox. Like most inhabitants of the area, she was a woman of few words. I offered her some coffee, which she gladly accepted. We women were left behind, stirring our cups, while the voices of the men, who left promptly to put up the stands, faded in the distance. We were both silent, and I could hear only the intermittent clinking of our spoons. I thought again of jokes I had heard about the mute cheer of the North Woods. This was exactly the way my afternoon with Edna seemed to unfold. The long silences were broken by my questions about her family and, in turn, by

Edna's pronouncements on hunting. Edna, who appeared to be in her midfifties, declared that she was tired of hunting because she did not want to climb trees anymore. I suppressed a smile, but I could see her point.

Edna commented on our bird feeder, which was being visited by numerous bluejays that day. With their tufts erect, they were standing in the feeder, as always thrusting their heads from side to side while, with their big beaks, picking up seeds and flicking many on the ground, where a new brood of chipmunks was eagerly waiting for handouts. After a while, the bluejays flew off, their beaks and cheeks stuffed with seeds. Edna declared flatly that they were robbers. They stole all the seeds, carried them off, and never remembered where they had stowed them. They were complete wastrels. She was completely deaf to the argument that through their apparent wastefulness the jays planted seeds and that they too served a purpose in the larger scheme of things.

She did not like squirrels either. They also plundered feeders. I agreed and candidly recounted how, the year before, Tom and I had caught half a dozen squirrels in our "Havahart" trap and deported them by canoe to the other side of the river. Edna looked at me sternly and, I guessed, with utter contempt. "But they'll be right back. They get on a log, swim, or just run across the river once it's frozen," was her answer. "I shoot 'em. They're good to eat, too. I shot one only yesterday," she added, "right out of my sliding window. I aimed right at it and hit it the first time around. I'll skin and cook it tonight." The flavor of my coffee suddenly changed, and I had to put down my cup. Was I too much of a wimp? Squirrels were so appealing. Small and reddish with white underbellies, they were amusing little animals. They seemed quite human when they sat on their hind legs and surveyed the goings-on. They seemed to look at you and talk.

Last year a mother with four babies nested near the cabin. We watched the babies grow. The mother brought them over one day, presumably from a different nest, higher up in a tree. One by one, she carried her offspring in her mouth, across the grass and up the spruce, where mother and baby disappeared. The tall, leaning spruce tree, still green in parts and producing cones, had a crevice through which, somehow, the squirrel family flattened their bodies to enter. Soon, the entire brood was safely tucked away.

The busy mother had her children stay put while she hurried down the tree again in search of food. I spent a lot of time watching the little squirrels peek out from their nest in the hollow tree, three, four at a time. The spectacle warmed my heart and made me chuckle. I loved how their tiny bodies, pressed together, hung out of the crevice. They made a shrill, rattling sound to mark their presence and warn away others. Their beady little eyes, dark with a whitish ring, looked at the world with curiosity. Then, within a week, they began to climb up and down the tree themselves. I watched them from the porch as they tumbled in the grass and chased each other through bushes and back up the tree again. I even forgot my irritation at last year's hole that we had stuffed up twice already with steel wool in response to the torn blankets and general havoc in the cabin. I marveled at the animals' agility. And they *were* cute.

Obviously, Edna did not share my opinion. She evaluated the squirrels from a purely pragmatic point of view. "You'll have trouble, squirrels are a nuisance," she declared, and that, for her, was final. Squirrels not only ate through wood, right into one's house, they also ate the seed reserved for birds and they deserved to be shot. They were, she repeated, also quite tasty. We never ventured to test Edna on the second point. Alas, she proved only too, too right on the first. When, a couple of years later, a squirrel family decided to move inside the cozy cabin for winter, chewed through beams, blankets, pillows, broke all the glass chimneys while possibly staging indoor races. The damage they did sorely tested my principles concerning the defense of animal rights.

Emma and I did not have time to pursue our topic that day, as the men returned from the woods. Tom was beaming. "We built two deer stands," he proudly announced. "One for you and one for myself. Amos said yours should be the one farther away so you would have to drag your deer a longer way." Laughter followed from all quarters, except from me—I found the joke quite tasteless. Amos reiterated that he would take care of the beavers, but only after the season had begun, in November, when the animals had their winter fur. Some people hunted beaver—illegally—in the summer. The inferior pelts were then sold as "fake fur" that city slickers were only too eager to buy. With these words, he laughingly bade us farewell and disappeared among the trees, followed by Edna.

More Beaver Stories

AMOS RETURNED AFTER THANKSGIVING on an old snowmobile that he parked in front of the cabin like a horse. He dismounted, removed his snowshoes from the rack, and signaled to Tom that he was ready to go. He wanted to visit the beaver pond now that the water was frozen and access made easier. Amos strapped on his old-style snowshoes, and Tom stepped into the bindings of his cross-country skis. I watched them as they set off across the snow-covered field.

Once again, as in the case of the car-towing episode with our neighbor Mike, Tom, who seemed so tough to our city friends after all this seasoning, still looked like he was newly arrived in the woods. Amos quickly strode ahead. Tom, in trying to keep up with him, lost his rhythm and plunged headfirst into the deep snow. I was following his maneuvers through my binoculars and roaring with laughter. He had completely disappeared under the white stuff. At first there was no movement. Then one ski tip appeared, and another; a head emerged, covered with snow. I could see poles waving in the air, and slowly Tom stood up with disjointed movements, looking like Charlie Chaplin with his cane. Amos stood there calmly watching, undoubtedly not without an inner grin. When Tom was back on his feet, Amos calmly moved on, with Tom stomping behind him on his skis. I followed the men until they disappeared between the trees in the midst of the snow and the cold haze.

Amos showed Tom where and how to set the traps. He decided, however, that Tom's wrists were not strong enough to open the traps. Tom laughed when he told me the story that evening. But before putting the traps in place, one had to determine if the beaver houses were "active." The gauge of this status would be a "chimney," a small opening through which the beavers aerated their house. If one saw warm air escaping into the atmosphere, it meant that the house was inhabited. An uninhabited house, that is, one without "smoke" coming out of it, had usually been deserted for lack of food or due to illness and death among the beavers. Both lodges on our property—the one in the woods and the one at the foot of our promontory—proved to be active, even "hyper-active," as far as we were concerned. It was still early in the season. Amos promised to come back and set the traps in a few weeks, just after the New Year when the water was really frozen and the beavers' pelts just right.

We were delighted. After several years of frustration, it finally seemed that we were getting nearer our goal. In a couple of weeks, we would at last be rid of the beavers! As the time passed before the set date, we no longer felt so euphoric. Poor beavers! We had watched them court in the spring and swim happily about all summer. And what would we do with all these beaver pelts? People up north tended to wear fur strictly to keep warm. We, however, lived most of our lives in a "politically correct" environment and could never wear a fur coat without getting hassled and harassed. A blanket would be too heavy. A rug was out of the question. Would the poor beavers have to die in vain?

We began to feel remorse about our murderous intentions and were glad we had some time to think through our dilemma. Further massive damage inflicted by the beavers along the shoreline and in the immediate vicinity of the lower cabin over the next couple of weeks did away with our moral dilemma. The beavers were now indiscriminately chewing on young aspens whose trunks were too slender to be nailed. I lay awake at night and thought I could hear dozens of beaver teeth chewing at the soft wood. This was it! Those beavers had to go.

Fate had it that at our annual neighborhood Christmas party in the city, one of the guests, a plumber, described a new beaver-eradication method devised by one of his colleagues. "All you do," said our friendly and well-intentioned neighbor, "is take a six-inch pipe, climb on top of the beaver lodge, and ram it down toward the center. This way, cold air will penetrate and the beavers will all freeze to death. That's the way my buddy did it." Detecting my reticence, he added, "It's not very nice, but . . ." He shrugged his shoulders and walked away to help himself to another canapé. Having overcome my reluctance to exterminate the beavers after their most recent transgressions, I was willing to shed blood and even to inflict limited torture. Let's try this method, I suggested to Tom, before having Amos come.

The following Friday we secured three six-foot pipes of various diameters to our roof rack and drove back up to our haven. The snow was already quite deep, and dragging the pipes into the woods proved to be no small venture. After much huffing and puffing, we arrived at the beaver house in what used to be a lush ash grove. Trees with the characteristic bite marks now seemed to stand even stiller in the frozen water. We walked out on the ice until we reached the lodge. From close up I noticed that it must have stood over five feet tall. Tom, imbued with the recent knowledge bestowed upon him by Amos, sniffed around. Yes, he said, yes, they're in there, I can see the vapor coming out of the chimney. I strained my eyes but saw nothing. I decided, however, that it was best not to doubt Tom's words.

Without further ado, we went to work. We both climbed up on top of the steep, snow-covered structure. I held one of the pipes erect on top of the lodge. Tom took a heavy mallet out of his backpack and proceeded to ram the pipe into the structure. *Bam! Bam! Bam!* The blows echoed in the silence of the frozen woods. Watch your fingers, I repeated, my motherly side coming out. *Bam! Bam!* Tom hit harder. The pipe did not budge. *Bam!* He tried again, straining his arm. "Son of a——!" He lowered his hammer. The pipe's ends were becoming dull from being hit by the hammer. We tried to look down the pipe, but the lower end was clogged with dirt and snow. The pipe's blocked, I objected. How can the cold air get through? Well, retorted Tom, I was told to hammer in one pipe, and once the hole was made, to remove the first pipe and slide in another, clear pipe. That way, the passage will already be open and no dirt will get inside the second pipe.

We decided to sacrifice the first pipe to make the hole and then insert one of the other two. Of course, we had chosen the smallest one to begin with and so would have difficulties driving in the larger ones afterward. We tried again. Tom's tired arms lifted the heavy hammer. *Bam! Bam!* The hammer glanced off the top of the –125– pipe. I screamed. "Watch my hands!" Tom offered an apology and resumed his banging, but to no avail. The method could work, but the ground was too frozen for any pipe to penetrate. We would have to come in the summer—with a canoe, I added jokingly.

We looked at each other and broke out laughing. Did someone play a joke on us? Here we were, trying to hammer a metal pipe into a rock-hard house built by big rodents. Our admiration for the beavers grew proportionately, and so did our ambivalence—until we looked around at the dozens of trees that had been, or were in the process of being, ruined. We abandoned the pipe project and waited for Amos.

Two weeks later, while we were up for a few days of skiing, Amos came to set his traps. They were not the leg kind, he assured me when he saw that I had some qualms. These traps led to death by drowning. The beavers would swim through a snag that made a clamp close. Without being "inhumane," a bizarre choice of words for the occasion, it was a quick death. For the time being, Amos chopped a hole in the ice with his ax and set the traps close to the beaver house in the river near the cabin. He would take care of the second and larger lodge later. He showed us the wooden sticks that were attached to the chains extending out to the traps and that he had planted in the snow. The sticks were now erect. When they leaned, it would be the signal that a beaver was in the trap.

The First Victim

IT WAS ONE OF THESE RARE LUMINOUS DAYS in late December. The air was bitter cold and still; the sky was deep blue and the snow glistened in the noon sunlight. The smoke from the chimney rose in a thin, straight line. In the morning we had gone on our skis into the forest. The river was becoming busier every year with snowmobile traffic, and we no longer felt safe there. Snowmobilers came up from behind you and zoomed by. They did not keep to the middle of the river, but liked to jump over the moguls created by mounds of snow-covered reeds along the shoreline. The machines approached with such speed that there was no way of escaping them. We decided to stick to our trails in the woods, where from time to time we could hear the high whine of another pack of snowmobiles roaring along the river.

It was the second day after Amos had set several traps in the river at the bottom of the hill in front of the cabin. After our morning ski, we checked on the sticks in the riverbank. One had tipped over. Was it possible? Could there be a beaver in the trap? Was it an optical illusion? Tom climbed down closer to the stick to make sure. The stick had been knocked over: there was a beaver in the trap.

Call Amos, I urged. Have him come at once. Tom made the call, and I could hear his side of the conversation. "Yes, yes, OK. Yes, we'll do that. We'll be right over. Yes, I know which turn. The first house to the right. OK!" I was not reassured. What now?

"Is he coming?"

"Amos wants us to bring the beaver to his house," was Tom's laconic answer.

I panicked. "But how? We don't have a snowmobile. How are we going to carry him to the car?"

"We just drag him in the snow."

"But we don't have a trailer."

"We'll put him in the back of the car."

This was Amos's revenge on us. He knew we were greenhorns. He wanted our nice vehicle full of fur and water. I complained, but Tom signaled that there was no time to waste. He climbed down the steep embankment, chopped a hole in the ice, and pulled on the chain. Through the hole, slowly, very slowly, the head of a great big beaver emerged. He was dead and already frozen. His long yellow upper teeth were clenched. Ha, at least this one would not chew down any more aspen trees! We had to enlarge the hole with the ax to remove the animal. The beaver was much larger than we expected—a good four feet long and at least eighty pounds. We put a rope on the metal trap and dragged the stiff body up the hill. We had to pause several times to take turns.

At first, we felt it was a macabre sight. We did not say much and felt queasy. Then, after a while, life got the upper hand. Death retreated, and we started trying to outdo each other with bad jokes. I impressed Tom by dragging the animal part of the way up the hill by myself. Then came the moment when we had to hoist him into the back of the car. I hastily spread a plastic sheet, and in went Papa Beaver, as we had dubbed him. We drove off to Amos's house with our first catch, which in the meantime began to thaw a little in the heat of the car and the afternoon sun shining in through the windows.

We sped down the highway to the intersection that led to the small town where Amos lived. The place looked like the set of a western. A few tall wooden buildings made of thin boards and crooked windows had been erected around a town square. Some Native American children were playing in front of an outdoor manger scene. A dim light shone in a small, empty-looking general store. It was Sunday, so the post office was closed. We asked the children for directions to Amos's house. They looked at us and ran off. Not a good beginning, getting lost in a town with four houses.

After going in circles for a good half hour, we chose the one street we had bypassed so far. We followed it for half a mile or so and had almost given up on ever reaching our destination when we spied a wooden structure in the distance. That was Amos's house. A few rudimentary steps led up to the door. To the left of the door, a couple of deer carcasses protruded from a cardboard box with the picture of a smiley, colorful Captain Morgan, mounted on top of a five-foot wooden pole. The meat left on the bones served as bird food. Nothing went to waste in this neck of the woods, Tom noted approvingly while I shuddered at the sight.

The door opened, and Amos stood there grinning. "Come on in, and bring your guest," he joked. Eager to please, we showed off our know-how. We each grabbed an end of the beaver, lifted him out of the car, and proudly carried him into the house. "Put him in the kitchen," Amos ordered. We made our way to the kitchen, where a small wooden table was ready to receive the beaver. We deposited our cargo with a sigh of relief, but we were far from done.

Following the local laws of hospitality, Edna invited us to sit down at the kitchen table, where we were subjected to the coffee ritual. An old kettle began to whistle on a gas stove. Edna made instant coffee in thick, white, diner-style porcelain cups and passed around a tin box of homemade oatmeal cookies. We slurped down our hot brew and chewed on the cookies, while two feet away from us lay the dripping beaver. We exchanged many meaningful glances. I had to cough several times to keep from laughing. Edna and Amos were passing around the cookies, pouring coffee, and making conversation about the woods, the weather, and the blooming African violets on the windowsill while the puddle under the beaver got bigger and bigger.

I furtively looked around the little house. The kitchen, with its big bay window, opened directly onto a sparsely furnished living room. It consisted mainly of a couch covered with a blanket and a small, fifties-style table with a scratched top. A few hunting and trapping magazines adorned it, with a couple of mail order catalogues from Gander Mountain. An old television set stood in a corner. A handcrafted antenna made possible the reception of the one channel available locally without cable. In the words of the advertisers, it was the channel "most Northlanders love to watch." Of course, most did not have a choice.

A lone painting in a cheap wooden frame, a discolored reproduction of Leonardo da Vinci's *Last Supper,* hung on the dark wood paneling. An unexpected sight indeed, especially as a backdrop for the beaver. On the opposite wall, several young adults in military

uniforms were smiling out from enlarged photographs. As with many other families of their generation, the Amos and Edna's children had left home by means of the army, the air force, and the navy. They were stationed all over the country and even the world. That was why Edna and Amos traveled around the United States. Last year, Amos explained upon seeing me glance at the portraits, they had gone to Texas, where one of their sons was stationed along the border with Mexico. To save money, they had driven straight through in their jalopy. It took them two days and one night. I quietly admired so much raw energy. They had been abroad as well. No, they did not like flying, but they had taken a stiff drink—against their habits—and that had enabled them to cross the ocean. They had been to Germany and Hawaii. Yes, I tacitly acknowledged, the world had gotten smaller.

Amos and Edna did not like that world. They had *their* world, and it was the woods. When we arrived, we had told the couple that we did not want to disturb them in case they wanted to go to church. "I go to no church," Amos declared. "My church is out there." He gestured once again toward the forest that began at his back window. "God has made all these creatures and all these plants. I like them, and I like it out there." Amos saw no contradiction between this statement and his trapping. He was a hunter and a gatherer. His clothes were worn until threadbare, his car driven until it stopped and could not be repaired. He was not part of the consumer society.

Like most Northlanders of their generation, Amos and Edna continued to live seasonally even though, in this area too, modes of production and shipping were beginning to relegate such a lifestyle to the past. They cooked, canned, hunted, cured, smoked, sewed. They ate their beavers and kept the skins they did not sell for their own coats and hats. They lived on a modest pension and were not the spokespersons of big companies whose headquarters were in glass buildings two thousand miles away. Yet they *were* trappers, and as such, they invoked the ire of animal rightists, including myself. I admired their resourcefulness and began to think about how I, as a wasteful city dweller, could claim the right to judge them.

When we arrived, Amos and Edna had been watching the local news. That day the newscaster, a friendly local man with a noticeable accent, baritone voice, horn-rimmed glasses, and a toupee, was relaying a report from a nearby mining town where a holdup had claimed several lives. "All this violence," Amos said. "Where is it all going? Too many guns, too much violence!" Clearly, for him, hunting and gathering was a livelihood, devoid of ritual violence, senseless killing and plundering.

"Want to see my atelier?" Amos suddenly asked, jokingly. He led us outside, past the deer carcasses. We scared up a few Canadian jays that flew into the nearby bushes, protesting at our passage. We entered a shack that served as a garage and beaver-processing station. Half a dozen beaver tails were hanging from a string stretched across the garage. Five or six pairs of what Amost told us were musk glands were suspended from wire coat hangers. Our festive mood evaporated. Was this a torture chamber? Amos explained that beaver tails, with their wrinkly skin, were used as fake alligator for shoes and leather bags. The musk glands were used in making perfumes, probably the very ones I was buying, he joked in my direction. I overcame my initial revulsion and upon Amos's insistence somehow got up the courage to touch, smell, and nod with approval.

Night was setting. It was only four o'clock, but daylight was short at this latitude. We returned to the main house, where a dim lamp was shining. Amos told us stories about animals and their habits. He was almost in tears when he told us of the wild turkeys he had introduced on a piece of property he was leasing and that were shot by some trigger-happy hunters from the city the year before. He also spoke out against the extensive logging planned for the region over the next few years. Too much logging, way too much. Because of it, there were too many beavers. It was the fault of monoculture, the absence of replanting, and greedy paper companies. Given this situation, the beavers had to be "controlled." And that was his job. He continued to philosophize on the animal world. Bears could not be trusted, bluejays squandered the seeds they took from feeders, squirrels were better in a frying pan than in either a feeder or an attic. Amos and Edna's frugal way of life, supplementing his meager pension by trapping and hunting, would be denied them by some groups in distant cities. I found the thought unsettling.

The first beaver from the river was soon joined by others, his wife and children, no doubt. More followed from the lodge deep in the woods. From fifteen pelts the local furrier made me a coat that I wore in the North Country, where, in twenty- or thirty-below weather and a severe windchill, few people stood around to protest fur coats. Most of us were just grateful for the extra warmth the furs provided.

A Silent Spring

MAY ARRIVED, AND ONCE AGAIN IT WAS TIME for our annual tree planting. Balmy winds were blowing from the south. Soon green leaves would spread a lush green coat over the naked branches of the tall aspens. Bushes would bud, and even the spruces would grow their bright green tips. The river was already open and flowing high. From the porch of the cabin, we looked at the greening field, the forest with the budding trees, and the vast expanse of the shimmering river. We cast some furtive, guilt-ridden glances toward the beaver lodge at the bottom of the hill. All was quiet there. Amos had done his job. He had pulled out more than twenty beavers from the two lodges on our land. With confused emotions, I contemplated the small waves lapping at the rotting logs on which the first grass of the season was growing.

It was around this time last year that we had seen the beavers playing and nuzzling on the log. I vividly remembered scenes from a previous spring, when, just after the ice had broken, two beavers, enjoying their first outing, had climbed onto a fallen log. I remembered their strange, whining noises and the way they had touched noses several times, obviously happy to see each other and to enjoy the spring air. Now, instead of being able to enjoy their first swim, Castor and Auric, sewn into a coat, were hanging in my closet, soon to be stored for the summer at the dry cleaners. I wiped away a remorseful tear. There were no tears when I looked in the opposite direction and saw shavings at the bases of chewed-up trees.

Farther out, many downed logs bore testimony to the beavers' erstwhile presence. Nonetheless, it would be a silent spring and summer without the familiar sound of beavers' tails slapping the water. We would surely miss the glistening V-shaped wake of beavers swimming upstream on a moonlit night. All was quiet and somewhat eerie. Oh, well. We tried to shake our memories and our guilt. Life goes on. Trees have to live, too, we convinced each other. Tomorrow we would even plant some more to replenish and, like good stewards, diversify the forest.

A New Plague

WE WENT OUT TO THE FIELD TO INSPECT THE PROGRESS
of the evergreens we had planted over the years. This was
the time of year when they were easy to spot. The dark green
color of spruces and red, white, and jack pines stood out in the
brownish yellow grass on which the last patches of snow had
melted only a couple of weeks before. In another week or so, after
the first rain, nature would truly explode. Tall ferns would unfold,
brush would fill in. The forest would take on its thick summer look
again. While thinking out loud, we measured the height of our
cherished pine trees and inventoried the damage done by winter
kill and hungry deer.

None of last year's "improved stock" of native white spruce had
made it. Our drudgery had been in vain. The slope where we had
planted them seemed cursed. Earlier, fired up by Tom's romantic
imagination, we had tried to grow some apple and plum trees in the
same spot. Our local friends had a field day. They were still snick-
ering at the mere mention of the words "plum tree," which Tom
did not take kindly. The tamarack seedlings were never to be found
either. They were so tiny that they were immediately covered by

grass, weeds, and shrubs. Only after a decade, and quite by chance, did we discover three sizable tamaracks that we had planted in the marshy part of the field. We choked with emotion.

Generally, the survival rate of transplants, taller and with longer root systems than the tiny seedlings, was good. Our endeavors were rewarded with visible results. The red and white pines especially had shot up in the field during the previous year. I was already dreaming of the day when they would be large enough that we could sit under them. I had always dreamed of a cabin in the "whispering pines." Yet for this to come true, it would take another twenty years or so. Our backbreaking efforts were worth it since we were reintroducing diversity into our forest, to produce real wilderness, or so we persuaded ourselves. Trapping the beavers would give the trees a chance.

Still daydreaming, I walked toward the cherished, large black spruces in the back of the field. Suddenly I noticed that the tips of the branches that, at this time of the year, were usually bright green and covered with a brown sheath, looked a bit thin, at least from a distance. I approached, somewhat alarmed. The branches, I discovered, were crawling with tiny worms that moved between branches by means of silky threads. The buds were being devoured. Spruce budworms, as we later learned they were called, were destroying all the evergreens. We were informed that they especially attacked spruces and balsams, and occasionally, red pines. They came in cycles, covered large areas, and stayed for at least two or three years. At the end of spring, after they had eaten all the new buds and metamorphosed into moths, they deposited their eggs into the ground at the base of the trees. They were no longer to be seen, leading one to think—or hope—that they had departed. Yet the following spring, they reemerged to strike even harder.

Spruces were hardy and could survive an attack unless the trees were old, fragile, or sickly. Balsams had a harder time recovering. Was there a remedy? Yes, we were told, one could spray them with chemicals. But how would we do this in the field, let alone in the forest? With canisters on our backs, we could treat a few trees behind the cabin, but an entire forest? These were some of the questions we addressed over the telephone to a forester with Department of Natural Resources, who provided no clear answers. The department had thought about spraying from an airplane, the official informed us. We eagerly accepted the idea and were ready to pay our part. We were going to save our trees at all costs. Armed now with canisters and masks instead of nails, hammers, and an ax, we stomped out to the field to rescue the two dozen large spruces, in addition to those that were growing in the immediate vicinity of the cabin. Triumphant, we thought we could claim victory.

The following year at tree-planting time, the trees were beginning to bud and no worms were in sight. They must have died thanks to our efforts and the long, harsh winter, I surmised, rejoicing. Wrong again. Two weeks later every tree in sight was crawling with worms. The DNR decided against spraying. When we pressed the officials, they were vague. They invoked cost and lack of feasibility. Only later did we realize that since so much of the area was slated to be logged, why would the DNR want to spray trees that would just be cut down? In fact, the disease conveniently offered an additional reason for cutting, to "ensure a healthy forest."

In its most virulent state, the plague lasted for three years. Most balsam trees as well as many of the old "granddaddy" spruces died. The dark, thick, mysterious grove of balsams that grew along the river near the swimming hole looked like the skeletons of Christmas trees that people put out for pickup in January. A fire hazard, I complained, angry and depressed. Indeed, the forest was tinder-dry after several years of drought. With the balsams and many of the spruces now dead in addition to the birches, it seemed that a spark would easily make it all go up in flames.

Urbanization

WITH THE ARRIVAL OF SUMMER, and under the illusion that both the budworms and the beavers had disappeared, we resumed our hikes, picnics, canoe outings, and daily swims.

The eagles were no longer the only ones flying over our heads while we indulged in aquatic pleasures. By law aquaplanes had to avoid the Boundary Waters Canoe Area Wilderness, so they flew over our area instead, just beyond the western perimeter of the BWCAW. "Wilderness" proper was steadily moving north. When we first bought our land, one bright blue aquaplane made one daily run, carrying mail and goods to and from the border post a few miles north of us to the first town twenty miles south. Over the years the planes had gradually increased until, one day, the traffic became quite noticeable. To the howl of snowmobiles at all hours during the winter was added the rumble of aquaplanes in the summer. This did not, of course, include the increasing number of passenger jets on their way to and from Boston, Seattle, Europe, Los Angeles, Detroit, Tokyo, and Beijing. At night, shooting stars rivaled speeding satellites. The Voyageur Highway, once confined to the rivers and navigable only during the summer, was now open year-round and extended far into the sky.

Not only was "wilderness" moving north, the concept itself was undergoing scrutiny. Was "wilderness" to be equated with unchangingness, with pristine nature? Or, did it go hand in hand with development and, if so, what kind? The area bordering the Boundary Waters, including our land (logged in the 1930s, as the aerial photograph on our porch kept reminding us), was, by the time Rob and Louise arrived in the 1970s, overgrown with pine, birch, ash and maple, but especially mature aspens. It was around that time that another idea of wilderness became desirable. A "return to wilderness" was now viewed, in addition to notions of "roughing it," as a more natural way of life. The idea was quickly marketed. Producers of various types of clothing and camping equipment, manufacturers of canoes and skies, resort owners, real estate agents, makers of off-road vehicles, all profited from the unexpected boom. By the time it was legally instituted in the early 1970s, the "wilderness" of −139− the north had already been heavily shaped by humans.

When we arrived, a couple of decades later, the future of this concept of "wilderness" was at the center of intense debate concerning not only the Boundary Waters but also the entire North Woods. There were those in favor of logging, and those who opposed it; those who advocated unlimited use of gasoline engines and the expansion of areas into which they could be taken, and those who tried to preserve "wilderness" and keep it quiet. Some argued for speed and development. Disputes over motorized access to portages and lakes in the Boundary Waters and on rivers such as the Vermilion divided local residents as well as regional and state officials. Businessmen pushed for motorized expansion both in and outside of the Boundary Waters, while idealists, nature lovers, and New Agers were more for preserving the purity of nature.

At least in our immediate area, most of the local population favored motorization, from four-wheelers to snowmobiles. It seemed they had just recently emerged from premodern ways of living and now wanted their share of modern conveniences. Some "tree huggers" protested, rather in vain. Over the years, slowly, another segment of the population would join the latter to inflect wilderness with yet another trend. City dwellers, in search not only of spiritual renewal but also fitness, looked for cross-country ski trails, mountain bike trails, and canoeing and kayaking routes. These people wanted to take in the scenery and see wildlife while staying fit, but were also reluctant to give up their "urban" ways. They looked for reconstructed "vintage" bed-and-breakfasts, cappuccino bars, and bagel delis with rustic log cabin decors. The more successful towns to the east such as Ely had quickly adjusted to new laws of supply and demand; others were slower to follow.

In our neck of the woods, the ideal of the gasoline engine continued to reign supreme. Snowmobiles abounded in ever greater numbers. The big furrows they made could be seen in the reeds throughout the summer. Where their skis raked the ground in our field, clover grew. At least they kept the grass down and made

for a sound walking or jogging trail in the summer, I muttered. The snowmobiles, no doubt quite unbeknownst to their riders, each year decapitated a number of small trees that were peeking through the snow, barely visible to the eye. Judging from their impact on flora, we wondered what they did to the wildlife. Surely, the fast-moving engines that kept us off the river must be doing the same for them. Many animals most likely took refuge in the forest. But what about the deer, the wolves, and other animals that liked to travel on the river? Some concerned local citizens had tried to pass an initiative to keep the snowmobiles off the river. It was narrowly defeated.

Jobs were the reason. Snowmobiles and logging meant business to local taverns, motels, and liquor stores. They kept alive a region that had been destitute for too long. With the end of trapping, fishing, and farming, with the collapse of the mining industries and the closing of taconite plants under the impact of imported steel, gasoline-powered tourism and logging were now considered the main road to prosperity.

The more ingenious of the local residents, abandoning logging, were beginning to build up their businesses around tourism. Whereas in Ely, "shoppes," "authentic" outdoor clothing and handmade furniture stores, and outdoor cafés with hanging planters were the norm, here styles were still confused. People tried to emulate their eastern rivals without quite knowing how to go about it. Eclecticism prevailed. In a nearby town, the first local McDonald's, with a thirty-foot golden arch towering over the white pines behind it, was inaugurated with great fanfare at a time when, nationwide, many franchises had begun building quaint little restaurants adapted to local architectural styles and changing tastes. History was being resurrected for tourists. "Voyageurs Days" featured colorful representations of bygone wilderness times that probably never were, complete with tents, trappers, Native American dances, tepees (though they were not really indigenous to this area), CDs with voyageur songs and books, live reenactments of encounters between Europeans and Indians, and the like. These "wilderness" spectacles came to replace the Harvest Moon Days that celebrated now less fashionable farming practices. The community catered to its own changing tastes but was not quite able to capture those of more affluent urban tourists.

So much gasoline-driven tourism with three-wheelers, four-wheelers, and even projected trails for dirt bikes, compromised our own idea of a wilderness adventure. An area farther down the river had recently been turned into a golf course in the hope of attracting retirees. At least it would keep our property values up, I sighed. The golf course had nine holes and belonged to a family that ran it out of an old tavern turned clubhouse. It was a strange sight indeed when, from our rustic cabins without electricity, running water, or plumbing, next to where beavers, bears, wolves, moose, eagles, and other animals still roamed, we emerged from the "Vermont road" and, a little farther down on the county road, spotted golfers in brightly colored attire (green-and-yellow Hawaiian shirts were the "in" attire one year, orange jerseys with two horizontal stripes another) swinging clubs, standing by holes, and discussing shots. Electric carts crossed the roads instead of the more familiar bear or deer. To keep the course green, the owners pumped water out of the river in the early evening hours. Now, when contemplating the sunset, we could hear the steady noise of the little pump's motor accompanying the warblers, frogs, and rustling leaves.

The general store in the nearest town, twenty miles west, where we did our shopping, after burning down in the winter—like many local businesses, for "unknown causes"—reopened in a larger, improved version. It was now a convenience store, complete with lottery tickets and the latest videos, the same as in any major U.S. city, and a fast-food corner where hotdogs turned on electric spits. The remaining old men with their John Deere caps, displaced from their bench overseeing traffic on the main road, competed for the yellow plastic booths with local teenage boys with shaved heads, baggy pants, and Calvin Klein T-shirts, and girls in long tight skirts. I knew that life in the North Woods had reached a turning point when, waiting in line at the checkout, I overheard a Native American woman who operated the local "Native Crafts Shop" inform the cashier that she had spent all day selling her products "on-line." The store also housed a laundromat and, the epitome of modernization, now allowed customers to pay with credit cards. That was progress. And it all had taken place in less than a decade. The changes brought the community money as well as, of course, an increase in petty crime.

At this point, human expansion also began to put pressure on fauna and flora everywhere. Local roads were being widened and resurfaced for easier access. Dirt roads were groomed and paved. One could now read the names of sponsors proudly displayed on road signs. Adopt-a-Road. Hunters' Paradise. The Voyageur Inn. Olsons' Outfitters. The roads were redone for tourism, but, just as the American interstate highway system had been planned for military purposes, so, as it would turn out a little later, they were also being expanded for logging on a massive scale.

The Beavers Return

I<small>F DAILY PLEASURES MADE US FORGET THE TRAVAILS</small> of the world at large, the latter were nonetheless knocking at the door. I was slowly relinquishing the idea of control in our little patch of paradise and reevaluating my concept of harmony and nature. Yet I felt we were still struggling against what I denounced as the unabated forces of chaos. Indeed, to what I continued to refer to as the earlier "destruction" by the beavers was added that by tent caterpillars, spruce budworms, and, soon, logging. We were being encroached upon by nature and by industry.

While some trees and bushes died of natural causes or had been the victims of beavers, others, like the alder bushes, spread and took over. They began to encircle the aspens along the creek. Impeccable strategists, they advanced individually, then by groups, into the open field. Along the river they first filled in the shore and then, like good soldiers, started to climb the hill. If, at least, the wood were worth something, we could cut the bushes and sell them, we sighed. That was some time before chic chain stores like Crate and Barrel began marketing "alder tables and chairs" as the latest in urban style.

On one of our strolls across the field, we had spotted some white splotches on the bushes. Having learned from experts that this was a fungus that spelled death for the alders, we rejoiced. The white fungus would gradually take over the plants, which would turn charcoal gray before slowly drying out and dying off. But contrary to our expectations, the alder fungus seemed to grow at a snail's pace, and even to reverse its course. I urged Tom to go out with his chain saw and thin them out. Giving in to my pleas, he spent several days sawing and making piles of brush. His labor hardly seemed to make a dent.

The next spring, when we arrived to plant trees, the alder bushes looked thinner. Winter kill, Tom suggested. He went out to do his chores and soon came back to fetch me. He guided me across "the lawn" in front of the cabin and stopped just beyond where brush had been growing. I stopped to take in the scene. It had been thinned, all right. A swath ten feet wide had been carved

out. The brush, mainly alder, had been razed. The opening passage began at the shoreline and went straight up the hill into a thicket, where it disappeared out of sight. The beavers were back, and they had taken down all of the alder bushes. O sacred and joyous beavers! What Tom had painfully and unsuccessfully tried to accomplish with a gas motor, the beavers had done for us the "natural" way. They were good neighbors. It was really great to have them back. How could we have been so foolish and so cruel as to have them trapped?

Both our enthusiasm and our guilt subsided somewhat when, following the steep trail, we arrived at an area where the beavers, left alone in the midst of winter, had cut down a healthy grove of young aspen, ash, and even birch that bordered the foundation of the old homestead. We were left feeling ambivalent, but our earlier antipathy had nonetheless dissipated, intensified by the discovery that the beavers had also cut down many of the alder bushes along the little creek flowing into the river. We felt quite sentimental about our precious little helpers. It did not immediately occur to us that the abundance of food assured the beaver population of a healthy and productive life, the consequences of which our trees would be the first to feel. At this point we were content with joking that the beavers were working for cheap furniture companies and mail-order houses and that they definitely had a sense of style.

Joe Ahearn

IN LATE AUGUST, WE WERE LINGERING at the breakfast table, watching the sun rise from behind the slender spruce trees beyond the bird feeder. The first rays were casting oblique shadows through the mist that shrouded the river and the nearby field. The mist was rising swiftly off the dark water with its glittering, golden streaks from the early morning sun. Gradually, as the sun rose, the mist retreated, first from the field and then from the water, on which the last air bubbles of the night still traveled. The mist eventually concentrated at the far bend of the river, where, in the valley of a little creek, it hung about while, under the brightening sky, the water took on the glistening blue that was part of the North Woods.

We were lost in thought when the telephone rang loudly. Tom came out of his reverie to answer the call and seemed suddenly wide awake. It was the local representative of Potlatch, the company that proposed logging along the eastern edge of our property. Tom, whose penchant is never to say no, much to my dismay agreed that the person come see us the next morning.

Joe Ahearn arrived at the appointed hour. A nondescript, dark-haired man in his midforties, he had studied forestry in the Northwest. He was knowledgeable about trees, soil, and the impact of logging. He had worked earlier for a small firm and had been laid off; now he worked for Potlatch. Although not insensitive to environmental concerns, he cherished his job. With a wife and two teenage children, Joe could not take chances. His responsibility was to secure logging rights from managers of public land or owners of private property with heavily wooded tracts. And he was relentless. Henceforth, if the telephone rang before seven in the morning, we knew it was Joe. After nine in the evening, there was also a good chance that it would be he. "Hello folks," he would say in a loud, friendly voice. "How are you today? Any decision? Not yet. OK, that's fine, take your time. No pressure, no pressure. Just wanna help you folks produce a healthy forest. Just wanna come by and talk to you a bit."

On the first day, Joe was there "just to talk." Since they would be logging behind our property, they could do ours at the same time. They would have to build only one road. Two in one. He carried with him ample literature. The company had outfitted him with glossy pamphlets that featured color pictures of friendly representatives who, like Joe, were talking with families in their living rooms. Everyone in the picture was smiling. Another image featured a family walking hand in hand through a forest of tall trees. The caption read: "Timber companies in the service of families . . . The text was intended to persuade readers that the thinning of trees was important to the forest's "good health."

The unspoken—and the unseen in the pictures—was, of course, that after the logging, there first prevailed utter devastation. The extent of the damage depended on the individual local logger hired by the company. Some left slash debris everywhere and literally gutted the forest. Others, more considerate, did not leave a battlefield. Yet everyone had to admit that it would take twenty or thirty years and more until the forest—unless it was replanted with genetically engineered trees—was back to a respectable height. It would take sixty or seventy years to achieve the effect in the pretty pamphlet

Joe Ahearn had brought us. Furthermore, some planting had to be done. The pine trees featured in the picture did not grow on their own. For them to do so, one would have to go through a long cycle, from the present human-induced monoculture to brush and then, finally, back to pines. Never again would the family that decided to have its forest clear-cut see trees as tall as the ones that had been felled. At least not the members of the present generation. The glossy picture was entirely misleading.

Joe answered questions but skirted real issues. He spoke firmly and was unperturbed by my counterarguments to his logic of the necessity of cutting the trees. Forests were vulnerable to fungus, he explained. In the past, fires had cleansed and renewed them. Now, because of Smokey Bear's watchful eye (he laughed, proud of his sense of humor), fires were rare. Nothing renewed the trees (except for the beavers and the worms, I thought); therefore logging was the most natural and necessary means to ensure healthy growth.

There was no arguing with Joe. He dismissed or pretended not to hear arguments for the necessity of fungus, or for replacing the expression "disease" with "another type of health."

Old trees, sick trees, leafless trees, I interjected, were equally necessary for the survival of many species of birds, beetles, rodents, and the like. Human policing broke these chains. To ensure diversity, habitat was needed. Soil erosion threatened water quality. Monocultures, the overabundance of aspens, led to an increase not only in deer population, which in turn helped the wolves. Beavers, I continued to advance, more and more aggressively, thrived unchecked. In a monotone, Joe reiterated only his point about the forest's health. He was a company man, intent on doing and keeping his job, and like a good diplomat, was trained not to argue.

"Jobs" were once again the main local argument for logging. The loggers had bought expensive equipment and needed to make their monthly payments on their loans. They reminded us of farmers in the southern part of the state who had resisted agribusiness with similar arguments. Just as, eventually, they had to give up their farms, so these folks would have no more trees to cut if everything went as planned. They were also at the mercy of corporate decisions. Other forests would eventually be found that were cheaper to clear, and companies would have no qualms about moving their business.

In the short term, the logging in the area seemed to bring a much desired prosperity. Potlatch was even talking of expanding locally. Forests in the area had not been cut in sixty years and were "ready" for harvest. Asked about the future, Joe merely replied that there was talk of bringing the waiting period between cuttings down to a forty-year cycle. Trees would be a bit shorter, he conceded, but big enough, healthier, and with fewer fungal problems, hence with less waste. This change in policy provided more jobs. "Well," he added, slurping down the last of his coffee that Tom had offered, "I hope you folks change your mind. I'm sure you will. Will you?"

He brought his body forward and, leaning over the table, eagerly looked at Tom. He already knew he would not get much help from me. But he still had hopes with Tom and was keen to talk to him "man to man." He had plenty of time, no pressure! The cutting along our property line would not begin until January or February of the coming year. It had to be done when the ground was frozen, Joe echoed Ralph Kahn, so that the bulldozers and the bunchers could easily get through tough and swampy areas. (Such as beaver ponds, I said to myself. This was one way of taking care of everyone's problems.) Some cutting had already begun, way back. He gestured vaguely. But our decision could wait for another couple of months. It would make sense to do it at the same time as the forest behind our land. "No pressure," Joe repeated, as he left. "We want you folks to make your own decisions."

When the telephone rang the following morning before seven o'clock, we did not have to guess who the caller was. And Joe would make his daily call until the end of our stay. Long after we had returned to the city that fall, the telephone kept ringing before 7. Joe had found our number and wanted to work on us some more. Other people often claimed not to be able to reach us. That was never the case with Joe.

Big Timber

❋

A FEW MONTHS LATER, THE DAY AFTER CHRISTMAS, we ventured out on our skis and decided to follow the loop that would take us through the forest, along the always partially open creek, over the beaver pond, through the stand of thick spruces, and, finally, down the gentle slopes among the tall aspen trees before we reentered our field.

We were laboring down the path that no hunters had groomed for us. A bad omen, I thought. We finally reached the point of bifurcation, from where we could either go straight and end up eventually on our treasured Blueberry Hill, or we could turn and follow the path across county land. We chose the latter and started on the path that first led through thick brush before it crossed the aspen and spruce forest along the creek where deer liked to roam. Tom was the first to emerge from the brush. I heard his startled "Wow!" and hurried to catch up with him.

We both stood there dumbfounded. Where there had been a forest of mature, tall aspens, spruce, and pine, crossed by a creek, emptiness and wasteland now ranged over several square miles. An eerie silence reigned. Somewhere in the distance, a piece of cloth was dangling from a forgotten tree trunk—the remainder of one of the deer stands from earlier times.

Once we had overcome our initial shock, we took a closer look at the ravaged forest. We saw not even stumps—bunchers did a much more radical job than humans—only overturned ground, with slash, broken branches, and here and there a trunk, usually of a rotten aspen that had been rejected more than spared during the operation. The space was unrecognizable and appeared much smaller.

Using the remains of the deer stands as markers, we could trace our familiar path up a seemingly steep and endless hill to the first beaver pond that was part of our "loop." Exposed and diminished, the area seemed obscene. It had lost its mystery, its many small bushes, trees, nooks, and hiding places. It was barren, thus offered to the sky. Wow, we repeated, wow! Then, indignation began to overtake us. Even though it was destroyed, we were going to follow "our path." We were going to do our loop amidst and over all the chaos.

First, we made our way through deep snow, over branches and −151− chunks of bark. When we hit the logging road proper, I commented on the "widening" of our beloved path. The defunct beaver pond, frozen in the winter, had been converted into a natural bridge. The active one had disappeared, bulldozed under during the construction of the road. That was one way of getting rid of the beaver problem. Good thing we gave all that money to the trapper, was my defensive reaction. Yet the new road was tough going. Rocks pierced through the thin snowcover and made gliding virtually impossible. Each time we put a ski forward, we felt the impact of the hard ground all the way up through our spines to our foreheads. Thump, thump, we advanced over the frozen terrain. There was no soft snowy surface to absorb the blows and muffle the sounds, and no chickadees to accompany us, hopping from branch to branch as we glided through the trees through which oblique sunrays danced.

The silence was broken by the coarse cries of a few ravens. Some of them were circling in the air ahead of us. Something must be attracting their attention. As we approached the area, first, a tuft of hair appeared on the hard, snowy surface of the road. Deer.

Gradually the tufts of hair became thicker and more numerous. A few drops of blood, then a trickling.

Finally, after rounding another bend, we scared half a dozen ravens that were feasting on the ground. As they flew up in the air under loud protest, the object of their feast became visible. It was the bloody carcass of a fawn, no more than a year old, that had met its end here. Tracks all around made it certain: wolves. The fawn had ventured out into the open space—perhaps it had even been driven there, out of the hiding places in the woods—and, with no protection from trees, had easily been hunted down. The bloody bones of the tiny rib cage pointed accusingly toward the blue sky. Many struggles were being carried out daily in the woods, but this one had been helped by man, I protested. We could see only tracks and urine marks. The wolves must have dined on it right there the night before. Perhaps they had even carried off a few pieces to their own offspring.

We continued our loop in a rather despondent state. Where the dark spruces had stood, only a few branches were left. On the far side, an even thicker and more impenetrable part of the woods was being leveled by a big bulldozer. We could not see the end of the logging road, so it was clear that what the official pamphlets referred to as "regeneration" or "reconstruction" would be going on for some time.

We pushed ahead on our devastated trail over hills and dales where we had skied in past years. Hunters had already built a stand on a barren hill. And life goes on, Tom declared, full of sarcasm. The absence of trees gave hunters excellent visibility all around; with their perfected equipment and scopes, they had an unfair advantage over the deer. We continued on along some of the ravines and over boulders, and we explored the no-longer-secret places where, earlier, on moss-covered ground and under thick spruces, we had gathered chanterelles and pine boletes. Still shaken by our experience, we reentered our forest, saved from destruction because of our unwavering resistance to the advances of Joe Ahearn, Big Timber's local representative.

Wolves

I N SPITE OF THE PRESUMED OVERALL WARMING TREND, the winter turned out to be one of the coldest on record. Many animals starved and froze to death; the deep snow made it harder than usual for them to move around. Some came out of their hiding places, closer to human habitation, in search of food and shelter. Wolves were spotted in open areas and struck fear in people's hearts, still part of the same mythology that for centuries had prompted fascination with the elusive *Lupus*. Over the past decade, we had occasionally heard the howls of a few wolf packs when sitting on the porch or coming back late from canoeing when the moon was already up. We had followed wolf tracks during our skiing trips. The previous December we had watched a lone wolf stealthily cross the river, and late this fall we had spotted another chasing mice in the field. Mainly, though, we had seen only lone wolf tracks in the field and along our paths in the woods. We had also found the characteristic droppings with fur in them, which we had sniffed and studied with the seriousness of experts.

A few weeks after skiing through the devastated logging area where we had come upon the remains of the hapless fawn, we were sitting in the cabin, lingering over dinner as a fire blazed in the barrel stove. The thermometer registered a steady twenty-five below; a full moon shone brightly on the nocturnal landscape; the air was crystal clear and still. Suddenly the crackle of the branches in the fire was interrupted by a distant howl. First one, then two. It stopped, then started again. It sounded like a dog's bark, but was deeper, longer, and more guttural. Now there was a chorus. We rose and tiptoed out to the porch. We silently opened the outer door and listened. The howling resumed. It was very near us and seemed to come from the frozen river. We grabbed our jackets and stepped out. We stood still, facing the river. It was so bright out we could have read a book. The outlines of the trees, both at the end of the field and on the other side of the river, stood out starkly against the moonlit sky.

We stood motionless, touched by the beauty of the night, when another howl sounded even closer, seemingly right in front of us. We peered out across the snowy surface of the river, between two spruce trees. As the howling ebbed, we heard a faint pitter-patter on the ice. Then we saw a shape detach itself from the shadows of the trees on the opposite side of the frozen surface. A wolf was trotting down the river, coming straight in our direction. He must have been sent by others to explore the area. He was completely silent. Only the regular crunch of his paws on the snow was audible. Either he had not seen us or he was not interested in us; he was heading downriver without even a glance in our direction.

Less than a minute had passed when, suddenly, there was more movement. Another shape, then two, three, four, five, six more shadows emerged from the dark of the trees on the far side of the river and followed almost in single file behind their scout. It was a stunning sight indeed. A still winter night, a bright, full moon, a few flickers of water condensation glistening in the air, and a pack of wolves eerily and silently walking right in front of us, without acknowledging our presence. We followed them with our eyes until they disappeared around the bend above the rapids. We lingered for a while. The wolves did not return.

It was not quite like accounts we had read of people traveling through the forest, followed by packs of wolves. Nonetheless, we had seen them. We were shaken, not by fear but out of awe. It had been a mixture of eerie sensation and passionate attraction. It had given us a rush, of the kind we had rarely experienced in our years in the North Woods. In a flash, all the tales came to our minds and enhanced the muffled sounds, the silence of the landscape, the inaccessibility of the animals, who proudly, silently, arrogantly moved past us as if we did not exist.

The following day we ventured out on the river. The wolves must have returned to spend part of the night right in front of our cabin. Tracks were everywhere. They zigzagged and crisscrossed along the riverbank. They led into the woods and disappeared up the steep hills. We spotted numerous urine marks, and, rounding the bend in the river, we found on top of our swimming rock another bloody carcass of a medium-sized deer, testimony of a nocturnal drama. The wolves had been hunting. And that night they did not go hungry.

We did not see the wolves again that winter. Although, with the severe cold and aided by all the logging, wolves had come in closer, they still managed to elude us. It was not until the next summer that Tom spotted one right near our mailbox, off the main county road. Lonnie and Mike, our neighbors reported seeing one scratching at their garage door. People were not receptive to wolves yet. The myths were still too powerful.

More Chaos

After discovering the mechanized devastation at the back of our property the previous winter, we did not venture out of our part of the woods for the entire summer. We came to celebrate more and more our "rugged" forest with its fungus-covered trees and overgrown "messy" look. I was no longer complaining about having bought a beaver pond.

It was not until the following winter that, on another cross-country outing, we decided to follow the forest path behind the cabin that led by the logged area. Now that our loop had been "wrecked," we decided to start, as in the past, by following our habitual path, but then, instead of turning right into what had now become a wasteland, we would continue straight. We would eventually cross federal land and, after climbing a steep incline, we would reach our Blueberry Hill, which, with its tall, almost first-growth marker trees, had over the years become our favorite lookout and picnic spot. At least, I repeated defiantly, no one would dare to tamper with this hill and its old trees. No bulldozer, I declared, would make it up there. Tom was less encouraging.

That morning, while we were doing our chores, emptying the

water, bringing in more wood for the stove, filling the bird feeder, waxing the skis, we heard the faint noise of machinery. It was hard to tell exactly where it came from. It must be north of us, Tom concluded, and we dismissed it. As we entered the forest and were chugging along, we could again hear the intermittent sound of a machine. It grew louder, then it suddenly stopped before starting up again. I was a bit disquieted. Tom seemed unperturbed.

We pushed through some deeper snow. In the absence of the hunters, who had not returned since the cutting, no snowmobile had groomed the path to make it easier for us. Like beavers, even snowmobiles had their advantages. The hunters now used the royal way, the wide logging trail. The grunts of our laboring and the sounds of my voice filled the air and made us oblivious for a while to the monotonous background noise of machinery. It was only once we had passed the fork in the path and were on the way to the hill that the noise resumed, this time much louder. It sounded quite near us now. Suddenly, I had a hunch. I surged ahead without another word. I reached the outpost of our land, where the surveyor had painted a big red X on one of our slender birch trees to mark the property line, and what I saw riveted me to the ground, speechless.

Where tall trees had stood the previous winter, there were now only lots of fallen logs. The earth had been eviscerated. A monstrous yellow bulldozer was maneuvering in the middle of what was to be the continuation of the logging road. It was driven by a solitary, dark-bearded man in insulated overalls, with an orange cap pulled down over his face. It was unclear whether he did not see us or simply did not want to acknowledge us. He may have had no time for a couple of cross-country skiers. He was busy shifting gears, moving the heavy bulldozer back and forth. The bulky machine was leaping forward, stopping, jumping back. It pushed out of its way spruces, aspens, leftover birches. Its thick treads squashed small boulders into snow and dirt and churned up the ground. In its wake, there was nothing but destruction. Where, in the past, we had skied while trying to avoid bending too many branches or stepping on young pine seedlings, and admired the ice sculptures made by frozen water that trickled down along the path, where we had paused under thick overhanging spruce branches and discussed the bedding places of deer and the tracks of other animals, now there was nothing but a moonscape.

The bulldozer was just beginning to climb the slope. No obstacle seemed too big for it. I had a gut reaction. I remembered reading about the people in the Amazon rain forest who threw themselves in front of bulldozers. I waved wildly and stepped in the direction of the machine. "Hey, you!" I shouted. The man ignored me and went about his business. "Hey, you, stop this! Can't you see what you're doing?" The bulldozer had turned and was charging the hill again. A few more spruces hit the ground. The cracking and thumping was too much for my overwrought nerves. By now I was screaming. The man paid no heed. He began to back up, and I had to jump out of the way so as not to be crushed.

Tom tried to reason with me. We'll fight it another way. The bulldozer had grazed our property line. It even looked, especially to me, as if it had in a couple of spots gone onto our land. "We'll sue them," I said emphatically. Some of the trees had fallen on our property. And was that not part of our land there, where the big spruce was lying on its side, its roots exposed like a wagon wheel? We would sue the company. The bulldozer had not lost a fraction of an inch, so close had it passed by. I thought again of throwing myself in front of it. "Let's not be dramatic," Tom kept saying. "Let's not be dramatic!" So I finally backed down, and, with a feeling of utter defeat, we turned homeward.

When we arrived at our city house, there was a message on the answering machine from Big Timber's representative. They were planning to extend the road, but because a sharp bend would make it difficult to extract the trees, could they use part of our land to cut a gentler curve up the slope? The message had been recorded in our absence. It was, fortunately for them, too late. Not hearing from us, they had moved ahead and put in the additional bend they had hoped to avoid. But in the meantime, our secret path had been destroyed. What else was to come?

"Nature's Ways"

THE COLD WEATHER LASTED WELL INTO SPRING, and the deep snow did not melt until early May. Many more deer died of starvation or became easy prey to hungry predators. They could not even nibble on our pine seedlings, covered by a uniform white mass. Not a single bird came to the feeder. Had they gone to more reliable sources in the area? Instead of the cheery twitter of little chickadees, only silence greeted us each time we stepped out of the cabin, interrupted at times by loud noises from the river, the sounds of expansion cracks.

Winter did end, however, with a bang in mid-May. There were still patches of snow when the weather changed overnight. The thermometer climbed into the seventies, and suddenly the death-like, eerie stillness was over. Sounds, colors, and smells filled the air. Nature exploded. It seemed as if, with this superabundance, it was trying to make up for the winter kill. Peepers could be heard once again by the thousands. Their chatter lasted throughout the night and lulled us to sleep. Later in the season, the few that survived long enough to grow into frogs would croak up and down the river, echoing each other in three-tone statements. *Oh, oh, ooh! Oh, oh, ooh!* they went without tiring. The third *ooh* was the lowest note in the series. The chickadees, though, were still nowhere in sight, and neither were the deer, except for a lone doe with her fawn. The pair had survived the hunt and the ravages of winter. Many trees also had died from the cold. But so had the budworms, we joked. Whatever the reason, the spruce budworms were, by and large, gone.

We toured the field and checked on our trees, in the midst of the hum of insects that were coming to life everywhere. The branches of the spruces were budding, seemingly free of worms. The winter had done it! Or perhaps they had simply run their course? We felt triumphant, although our victory was mitigated by the fact that few balsams had survived the ordeal. Neither had many of the granddaddy spruces, as the forest specialist had called them. But young trees were already growing, healthy as ever. With great amusement we remembered how, only a decade ago, we had been so intent on preserving the status quo and even on constructing a pristine wilderness. Clearly, nature was in the hands of fates beyond our control. In addition to catastrophes like forest fires, now also known to be beneficial to many species, there were invasions of caterpillars, worms, grasshoppers. Some trees died, some survived, yet others thrived because of the demise of their competitors. With the balsams dead, ashes began to grow in great numbers near the water. It seemed as if entire groves were springing up out of nowhere.

Something was always growing, and the landscape was constantly changing. In addition to marked changes in flora and to some extent in fauna, the bank on our side of the river was pushing farther out into the water, while the bank on the other side was being eroded. Along the edge, the balsams killed off by budworms were beginning to lean over before gradually falling into the river, where they would provide shelter and access for animals. Fish liked to rest in their shade. Turtles enjoyed sunning on them. Ducks rested there. Larger mammals like beavers, fishers, minks, and bears used them for climbing in and out of the water. Similarly, dead or rotting trunks in the forest sprouted mushrooms and provided shelter for rodents as well as for insects. What some humans called an "unhealthy" forest was crucial for many species. Dead branches were extremely sought after by birds, from chickadees to eagles, kingfishers, phoebes, waxwings, and a whole array of woodpeckers. The branches of the large dead aspen in front of our cabin were, after a decade, so worn by bird claws, they looked, we liked to joke, as if they had been polished. The argument for "health" was clearly artificial and promoted to justify control by humans.

As if to counteract damage from the severe winter, nature ran riot in the fields and forest. Flowers covered the field with dense splotches of white, pink, purple, and yellow in turn. The daisies in June, the asters and orchids in July and August, and especially the goldenrod toward the end of the summer bloomed in profusion. Raspberries and blueberries abounded.

Not a single bear showed at the cabin all summer. It was not that they had frozen in their dens, but berries were so plentiful there was no need for them to come around human habitation. Berries were complemented by hazelnuts. In previous years, a sparse crop was all but gone by the time the nuts matured and turned brown, plundered by deer and bears. This year, Tom, who was the major nut gatherer, could barely make a dent in the abundance. I always opposed the picking on grounds that the nuts should be reserved for animals. The more I opposed it, the more Tom became obsessed with collecting them. The nuts were tiny and the harvest had more of a symbolic value. Tom liked to bring forth his survivalist side. We by now had deer meat, wild rice, beaver jackets, jam made from berries, teas from leaves and roots, so why not nuts? Playing on "nuts" I uttered some unflattering remarks. Unfazed, Tom escalated his drive for living off the land. Soon, the yearly crop of pine boletes and chanterelles would be added as well. A couple of French friends, after a recent visit with us, went back to Paris to declare: "We thought we were in a trapper's house!" I was alarmed, but Tom was amused.

At the end of the day, after our chores were done, we sat in our Adirondack chairs on the promontory overlooking the river and watched the night fall. In good years, that is to say, when there were not too many mosquitoes, we could sit out here and sip, depending on our moods, coffee, beer, wine. As the sun was setting between the trees in the west, we watched the river come to life. This was the time of the day when, usually, the wind died down and the water became calm and smooth.

It was also beaver time. Castor and Auric, the new tenants in the river lodge, "sailed" around half past seven, right under our eyes. They swam straight out in the river, then turned and floated, motionless, ears and eyes above water, tails extended, looking like logs. We sized up one another from a distance. At times, when we spoke too loudly or moved too abruptly, the beavers slapped their tails on the water to alert each other of impending danger and took a dive. We could see only their hind legs stretched up in the air and their broad tails. It would be a while before they returned to look at us again with a mixture of curiosity and suspicion.

I had some lingering ambivalence toward the animals but generally felt, like Tom, that they had become our friends and allies. They had gotten rid of our alders, and their efforts at felling a couple dozen trees seemed rather harmless next to the clear-cutting of hundreds and thousands of trees that was taking its course behind us. We now simply let them be in the forest. Echoing Jim Rondeau, we reassured ourselves that after all, this was wilderness. At least whereas the machines eradicated it, the beavers produced, albeit slowly, true diversity in the wilderness.

Glasses in hand, we were still philosophizing when a couple of stars appeared. Venus was always the first. Straight across the river, above the dark tree line, the planet shone brightly in the still-light sky. Soon the entire sky was studded with stars. We tried to impress each other by identifying them. The Big Dipper was a good point of departure. We could also identify the Little Dipper, the Pleiades, and Orion; but we did not get much beyond those. We should buy a guide to stars, we reminded each other. When the moon was full, it rose as a bright orange ball behind the trees at the back of the field. It looked menacing while it gradually wound its way across the field, just above the tree line, before it climbed up into the sky. The man in the moon, clearly outlined, seemed to greet us with a smile.

Back to Blueberry Hill

Six months later, as if drawn by a magnet, we decided to hike up to our Blueberry Hill, despite the fact that we would have to cross the "lunar landscape." Making our way down the narrow, dark forest path, we no longer glanced in the direction of the beaver pond but directly opposite, toward the area of devastation. Saplings were growing there, true, but we reminded each other that it would be decades before those aspens would be at a reasonable height again. With little replanting being done, the aspen monoculture was, at this point, guaranteed supremacy. We continued to follow the bulldozed path, where rocks were lying bare and slash was strewn about. We climbed over a first hill and followed a narrow, overgrown trail along a defunct beaver pond. Gone were the remains of the trapper's cabin, and so was his spring. We reached the bifurcation where we turned once again to climb Blueberry Hill proper. We fought our way through the hawthorn and hazel brush, getting stuck on branches and thorns before we emerged onto the large rock from where the steep hundred-foot climb began. We paused and looked up, as we always did. A split second, followed by the cold realization: all the gorgeous pines were gone!

Not one pine tree was left standing, save two marker trees and a couple of very young pines. We stared at the empty, rocky hill; we even forgot to breathe.

I was the first to break out of immobility. I ran up the hill, reached the top, and looked around. Everything was barren. Only a few branches on the ground bore witness to the massacre that had taken place. I felt like weeping.

Most of the trees must have been over a hundred years old. They had been home to nesting eagles. In their undergrowth had hunted wolves. The carpet of blueberry bushes beneath had been the pantry for many bears. The songbirds that darted among the branches would have to move. One hundred twenty-five was the magic age for trees to qualify as old growth. Any decision to designate an area "old growth" depended on the density of 125-year-old native trees and the size of the stand. A mixed forest would not qualify. Perhaps there had not been enough "density" on this

remote hill, or, we surmised, the feeling prevailed that what was out of sight would be out of mind, except for the steely-eyed gaze (assured by satellite or aerial photography) of the logging industry. Clear-cuts like this one were happening in more remote areas all over the north without drawing much attention or argument. Bordering on federal land, most of what had been logged had belonged to the county. The latter, in need of money, sold the logging rights to monolith timber companies intent on profit rather than the quality of the forest. The county put the land up for sale a couple of years later.

Why did people become sentimental about an animal, a cat, a dog, perhaps a mink, or a beaver but not a tree? Blueberry Hill would not regrow in our lifetime. Not even our children or grandchildren would see here mature white pines under which deer slept, bears gorged, moose ambled, and whose energy we felt so intensely.

Epilogue

I NEVER FOUND IN THE NORTH WOODS the long-sought adventures of my childhood heroes Chief Winnetou and Old Shatterhand. I never found what I thought was the harmony advocated by more modern writers. I discovered, however, that every order is fragile and that harmony is fleeting. During a decade in the North Woods, I came to change my views of nature and the forest. Not only did the stories of my childhood belong to another world, but my vision of harmony and peace was challenged every day. What I encountered in its stead was a nature rife with force, and that force was embodied in beavers, insects, and fungus. To salvage at least one of my earlier visions, I had at first tried to achieve my ideal by, paradoxically, exerting control. That approach quickly went out of control. The beavers moved, the caterpillars and the budworms attacked, and floods and droughts did the rest. In nature an unpredictable element would always reign.

As if to mock human attempts to control the wilderness, one Fourth of July, a storm ravaged the entire North Woods when, by extraordinary coincidence, two systems came together to produce ground winds of more than one hundred miles per hour. The storm hammered a swath several miles wide, flattening cabins, snapping trees like matches, smashing eagles' nests to the ground, and demolishing the homes of countless other animals. In some areas, trees were piled so high, they choked creeks and even lakes, killing off fish.

Inside the confines of the Boundary Waters, the storm led to another controversy, namely, how to deal with the damage when gasoline-powered means of intervention were illegal and when nothing could be touched in the area. The effects of this event would no doubt someday be exploited as a tourist attraction. People would come to see these new forest paths bordered by stacked-up wood. So much wood was left to rot, so much was lost.

"Wilderness" did not mean just peace and harmony. Nature was an ever-changing force field full of unpredictable elements. It was chaotic, and its very messiness often served a purpose. Yet, "change" was not solely the product of nature. It could also be induced by humans. Clearly, nature underwent the most serious changes through the hands of a rapidly accelerating human encroachment and intervention. Monocultures, carbon monoxide, acid rain, and population pressures changed growth patterns and affected plant and animal life in dramatic ways. Our bout of interference with the beavers had shown that control in one area brought about excesses in another. I emerged from our adventures in the North Woods with a wiser love for the beavers, who no longer struck me as the "nuisance animals" they had become through man-made changes, thereby joining the rapidly growing list of bears, deer, pigeons, gulls, and many other species.

I remembered the German philosopher who wrote of forest paths that lead nowhere, or perhaps, only to a clearing. For us these forest paths were now logging roads and they led to the next clear-cut. And while it was true that such damaged areas could also be produced randomly by a fire or a storm, these had been done quite calculatedly. In a certain sense, the logging industry too had its vision of harmony. Its argument of the healthy forest joined my vision of a manicured nature. To do so, it surely left no stone and no beaver pond untouched. It seemed, however, that where beavers' logging operations had an order in the greater scheme of things that led to diversity, human operations often led to simplification.

No doubt, many of the logging paths would soon be advertised by pamphlets at the official stations of the Department of Natural Resources as recreational, for mountain bikes, four-wheelers, snow-mobiles, and the like. It would enable tourists to have access to the forest. The only problem was, there was no forest left, so to speak. When admiring stars in the early morning hours or canoeing in the evening on the misty river while taking in the wilderness reflections, we noted that the cry of distant loons or the occasional howl of wolves—let alone the eerie nasal sound of the beavers—were lost to the deep and ongoing rumble of the logging trucks and heavy ma-chinery. Gift shops would have to update their official soundtracks for the North Woods wilderness experience.

While changes produced by nature and culture were inevitable, it became clear that every order was complex and fragile. Any changes had ripple effects. Far better to proceed with caution than to produce harmony by imposing an order. The war against the beavers and our years in the North Woods had taught me the art of treading lightly.

VERENA ANDERMATT CONLEY teaches in the Literature Program at Harvard University and has written about ecology, technology, and feminism. For many years, she and her husband, Tom Conley, have owned and enjoyed land on the Vermilion River in northeastern Minnesota near the Boundary Waters Canoe Area Wilderness.